"Over 33 million people li[...]se people matter to God. Yet you'd never know it by reading the books and attending the conferences aimed at church planters. It's all about the cities. It's as if small towns and the people who live there don't exist. Donnie Griggs has written an important corrective with passion, steely logic, and powerfully practical insights showing that small towns not only matter to God, they should matter to us."
Larry Osborne, Pastor & Author, North Coast Church

"The neglected rural back roads of America are the new frontier for church expansion and multiplication. Donnie Griggs is one of the trailblazers showing the way. Small Town Jesus is must reading for every pastor and church planter who want to make a difference in small town America."
Jim Tomberlin, Founder/CEO/Author MultiSite Solutions

"Donnie Griggs sounds a clear call for the necessity of planting and revitalizing churches in small towns with humility and courage. As a fellow pastor of a small town, I found myself quickly turning the pages and shouting, "Finally!" I enthusiastically recommend Small Town Jesus as the go-to guide for planting and revitalizing churches in small towns. "
Benjamin Durbin, Lead Pastor of The Bridge Community Church in Leadington, MO

"God has given Donnie a vital message for the Church. He has not just got ideas about reaching small towns for Jesus - he has seen amazing fruitfulness in putting those ideas into practice on the ground. Buy this book. Read it. Then read it again."
Phil Moore, Leader of Everyday Church London and author of "Gagging Jesus", "The Bible in 100 Pages" and

the "Straight to the Heart" series of Bible commentaries

"I know this man. I know his church. I know his town. And I wholeheartedly recommend this book to you. It will boost both your faith and knowledge to see Jesus do a big work in small towns...and big cities for that matter."
PJ Smyth, Leader of the Advance Movement of churches

"The forgotten America of the small town hasn't been forgotten by God and must be remembered by the church. Donnie's book will help us remember. This book is a great tool in the fight to build a church planting vision as big as the great commission."
Josh Kouri, Lead Pastor of Frontline Church, Oklahoma City, OK

"Donnie exemplifies what it means for a pastor to be a missionary and through this book, has brought much needed attention to small towns. I think this is a must read for anyone who is currently in or is thinking about pastoral ministry in any context. As I read it, I was confronted with the truth how I overlook areas of need because of what I see as important instead of what Jesus sees as important. Small Town Jesus inspires and equips to build gospel-centered churches where there is great need."
Bryan Mowrey, Lead Pastor of Jubilee Church, St Louis, MO and Midwest Regional Leader for Newfrontiers USA

"We need men who want to be known in their city more than they want to be known for their city." This is one of the most profound things I have ever heard and it was spoken by a man who embodies it. Donnie Griggs loves Jesus and has a grand vision for what a Big Jesus can do in small towns.

Much like an afternoon fishing with Donnie, Small Town Jesus will fill your heart with joy and confront your soul with conviction at what Jesus can do when we trust Him."
Brian Lowe, Network Director Acts 29 US Southeast

"For a number of years, I've encouraged my friend Donnie Griggs to write this book. Now that I've read it, I'm thrilled he did. It exceeds my high expectations. It is a helpful and necessary book for pastors, church planters, and those training for the pastorate, no matter the location of their church."
Elliot Grudem, Founder and President, Leaders Collective, Pastor for Church Planting, Vintage Church

"In an era when urbanization is a trend capturing the imaginations of politicians, business and cultural leaders, it is easy to forget that millions of people still live in small towns. The church can forget this too, with mission to the cities often presented as the only legitimate place for ministry, especially church planting. Donnie Griggs has bucked this trend, moving from a city to a small town and planting what has become a large church there. In this practical and inspirational book Donnie encourages us to have a more biblical approach to mission - one that does not dismiss mission to the cities, but which does include church planting in small towns. With wit, honesty and examples from his own experience, Donnie helps us see the significance of small town church planting, and gives us a roadmap for going about it. If you are already in a small town you should read this book and be encouraged. And if you want to be involved in church planting you should read it too - perhaps God wants you in a small town, not just to cut your teeth before going to the city, but because Jesus loves small towns as well as cities!"
Matt Hosier, Lead Pastor of Gateway Church in Poole, England; contributing author for Think Theology

"Numbers matter; numbers aren't just numbers, they represent children of God. Jesus came for these "numbers." It's staggering to hear, Donnie Griggs and One Harbor Church are reaching more than 1,000 people each week in a town of just over 9,000 people. This is a Jesus glorifying accomplishment, one that every small town pastor should strive for and one that every city pastor can learn from. This is a superb book that will help the church reach 33.7 million people in small town America or wherever you are!"

Tyler Jones, Lead Pastor of Vintage Church, Raleigh, NC

Small Town JESUS

Taking the gospel mission seriously
in seemingly unimportant places

EverTruth
Damascus, MD

Published by EverTruth
26700 Ridge Rd
Damascus, MD 20872

Cover design by Ryan Marshall

Unless indicated otherwise, scripture quotations are taken from the Holy Bible, English Standard Version.

Paperback ISBN:978-0-9914030-5-9
eBook ISBN: 978-0-9914030-6-6

ACKNOWLEDGMENTS

This book is dedicated to my wife Jill who willingly packed up her life after growing up in Southern California and joined me on this adventure of planting One Harbor Church in the small town of Morehead City. We wouldn't have come if you weren't willing to walk away from a lifetime of closeness to family and friends. Thank you for saying yes and trusting Jesus alongside me!

Special thanks to Rachel Shenk, Matt Castagna, Keith Welton, Andrew Haslam, Ryan Marshall and others at One Harbor Church for helping with editing of this book. I could not have done it without you. Also, to my friend Elliot Grudem, who was the first to push me to write about this.

TABLE OF CONTENTS

Part One

WHY SMALL TOWNS MATTER

CHAPTER ONE

THE SMALL TOWN PROBLEM

"Got nothing against a big town...
But my bed is in a small town
Oh, and that's good enough for me"
- John Cougar Mellencamp

This song by Mellencamp is one that most people would not only know, but would sing along to. It conjures up fond memories for many of us. If you're from a small town and now live in a big city, I bet you really enjoy this song when it comes on the radio. Even though it came out in 1985, "Small Town" is still a song most people really enjoy. He isn't ranting about how terrible cities are. He's just giving some love to the small towns and describing so many of their positive attributes. He seems to have a balanced love and respect for the cities and the small towns.

This is exactly what I think is missing in the modern

missional church landscape. Small towns have all but been forgotten by many people and by many churches. Big cities are seemingly where God is really moving. Is that right? Is that biblical? If not, what kind of damage are we doing with the insistence on urban centrality? Maybe we should be acting a little more like Mellencamp here than we are. Maybe we should be showing love and respect to both cities and small towns.

In America, this perspective of remote and sparsely populated areas is not new. In fact, we even have a word for it, "Podunk." It's a word whose origins date back to the Algonquian Native Americans who used it to describe people who lived in remote marshy locations. Even back then, they noticed that some people chose to live in areas where not many people would, separated from the main population.

Then in the early 1900s, "Podunk" became America's favorite humorous way of describing people who lived in small towns. They were commonly portrayed in literature and theatre as being backwoods hicks who had lost touch with the progress of the world. Eventually, this became such a popular way of thinking about small-town America that the word found a place in our dictionaries.

"Podunk"\'po-,denk\ noun: a small, unimportant, and isolated town - Merriam-Webster Dictionary

In our day, we don't use "Podunk" as much anymore, but the attitude of considering small towns as isolated and unimportant is still there. In a lot of places I go, there seems to be a love for the cities and a disdain for the small towns.

Added to this, mainstream society doesn't really understand small towns. What they do seem to know makes them suspicious, and even fearful to some extent of the people who live there.

Sound like I'm exaggerating? Just think about it. We view the cities as the best of culture, food and fun. However, the small towns are seen as places that may be worth visiting or pleasant to pass through, but little to no consideration is given to living there permanently.

At worst, many people view small towns as full of people who speak with funny accents and lack education or dental hygiene - where bigotry and racism are not only acceptable but are lovingly woven into the fabric of their culture.

Maybe this is because small towns lack the modern

conveniences of our favorite chain restaurants, shopping malls, and hip coffee shops. They aren't where the most current bands come to play. Most of them don't even have a movie theatre... that doesn't leak when it rains.

Regardless, it certainly seems as though small towns are not much of a priority to anyone anymore. Even politicians and statisticians are seemingly uninterested. As Princeton Professor Robert Wuthnow states:

> Relatively little research has been devoted to small towns since the 1950s... small towns were viewed as part of a declining sector populated by fewer people, and of interest more as the location of food production and tourism than as places where people still lived. As a result, data has been available from census reports about the number, size, demographic composition, and economic characteristics of small towns, *but little effort has been made to learn what residents of small towns think and believe.*

Out of sight and out of mind would be a good description of the mindset most people share regarding small towns. We don't think about them anymore, at least not in any way that carries sincerity.

What I mean is that, if we do think of those living in small towns, it's not a serious or genuine consideration of what kind of people comprise the culture or what values they share. We often classify them with gross stereotypes that in no way accurately describe the people who call a small town home. Wuthnow, commenting on this in America, continues:

> Two contradictory images of small-town America emerge. One is a nostalgic, almost bucolic view in which towns and villages are dominated by warm, neighborly relationships. The proverbial stranger who comes to town finds the townspeople at first a bit parochial, but then discovers them to be thoroughly good-hearted. The other view presents the small town as a place to leave as quickly as possible. The townspeople are unhappy, inbred, and reluctant to let go of the heroine who knows she must exit. The stranger who arrives is caught in a spiral of deceit and intimidation that cannot be escaped soon enough. *In either case, the town*

serves as a convenient setting in which to tell of drama and intrigue, but there is little information about what the inhabitants of small towns are actually like.

Essentially, small towns are valuable for our entertainment, humor and vacation. They serve as a good setting for romance novels or horror movies but are otherwise unimportant. The data available to understand small towns is useless to us because they don't make popular culture. They aren't where the famous and elite people want to live full time.

Having been born and raised in a small town in Eastern North Carolina, I would concur with Wuthnow's findings completely. Where we live is a place people love to visit for vacation. The way people talk "Down East," as we call it, is seen as humorous. A town right next to mine was famous for coining the term, "Freedom Fries" as a way of protesting the French for not supporting American military action after 9-11. And, funny enough, Nicholas Sparks, the famous author, lives just down the road and so our area serves as a beautiful backdrop for many modern romantic novels and chick flicks. We fit all the modern profiles for small towns in

America.

Again, none of this is really new. Even back on April 19, 1919, sociologist H. Paul Douglass noted in *The New York Tribune* that the popular opinion of small-town America was that, "God made the country, man made the city, but the devil made the small towns." Essentially, small towns were like "hell" to live in either because they lacked the progressive options of the cities or because those who lived there were perceived to be backwoods idiots.

As Goes The Culture, So Goes The Church

As it so often does, the church seems to follow behind the culture's positions and opinions. It just usually takes us a while. For example, the church was the last to fully buy into music with drums and dancing, but eventually we conceded. We didn't like tattoos either but now we're lined up at tattoo shops getting our favorite bible verses inscribed or a black and gray portrait of a Protestant reformer. The Internet was only the devil's playground until the church finally saw it as an opportunity to make much of the gospel...or sell bibles autographed by televangelists.

In the same way, it wasn't enough for mainstream culture to decide to look down on small towns; the church had to jump in too. In many places I go, Christians have seemingly bought fully into the belief that the city is where God exclusively wants us to be and where God is really moving. Many Christian leaders seem to look with disdain and snobbery at any attempt to justify the legitimacy of small town ministry. The widely accepted logic goes that if the gospel is received in the cities, the country's nooks and crannies will eventually be changed by Jesus too.

However, there are lots of important questions that no one seems to be asking. Questions like, is this exclusive attention that has been focused on the cities even the right thing to do? What are the consequences for our modern attitude towards small towns? What did Jesus actually do and does that mean anything for us today? What does this way of thinking communicate to those who presently live and minister in small towns, not big cities? How should people who do live in small towns understand their culture and engage it with the gospel? How do we hope to envision the next generation of ministers of the gospel who will end up in small towns if all we do is talk about the city? These are a few of the questions I hope to tackle in the pages ahead.

Why Is This Any Of My Business?

Why am I so worked up about this in the first place? Offering some context, with the exception of five years I spent living and working in a church in Southern California, I have grown up and lived most of my life in small towns in North Carolina and Texas. Specifically, I was born and raised in coastal North Carolina in a small town called Morehead City. I lived there until I was eighteen and loved every minute of it. Then I moved to Texas where I spent four years working at a para-church ministry in the middle of nowhere; the kind of place where there's only one blinking stoplight in town and everyone knows everyone.

However, I really only fell in love with church planting when I was in a great church in Southern California. I lived in Pasadena and in Fullerton. It was there that I began learning about the centrality of the gospel and the importance of mission. Honestly, I too felt that if I ever did plant a church it would have to be in a large city somewhere in the world. I considered everything from large beach cities in

Southern California, with a mix of pure and impure motives, to places around the world a little less comfortable. However, all of the places I envisioned myself were huge.

To be even more honest, upon realizing God was leading me to come back to my hometown and plant a church, it felt a bit strange. It almost felt wrong. It felt like maybe a part of me was compromising, selling out or stopping short of the fullness of my potential. How's that for arrogant? We'll get to more of that later.

The question that kept coming back to me was, why would God want to call my wife and I to plant a church in such a small, remote part of the country? Why leave the over thirteen million people living in Los Angeles and Orange County for a tiny little town most people have never heard of?

The place God was calling us back to was my hometown, Morehead City. Morehead now has just over 9,200 residents and our 1,300 square mile county has a population just over 68,000. It's not a big city by any stretch of the imagination, but what I've come to see is that the people here are amazing and in need of Jesus as much as any big city inhabitant.

Truthfully, we moved because we felt God say so. It didn't make sense to us then, but it makes a lot of sense to us now. It has been absolutely astounding to see how Jesus has poured out his love and goodness in our small town. With meager beginnings, our church started in a living room with a handful of friends seven years ago. I do not know where to begin to describe what God has done since then. I will say this, he far surpassed any realistic expectations I had for the future of this church, and the impact has been real, enormous and has been felt by all walks of our community and beyond.

To continue painting the picture, One Harbor Church, the church we started, now has over 1,000 in attendance every week. We currently have three sites and are already working on our fourth in a neighboring small town. Beyond that, we dream of planting churches or sites all up and down Eastern North Carolina.

We have seen what any church planter anywhere hopes for. Marriages are being restored, people are seeing their jobs and hobbies as opportunities for mission and we routinely witness God saving people who others had written off.

Looking back now, I'm embarrassed when I remember that my expectations were that one day we may have thirty or so people meeting in a living room...if we were lucky. I am totally blown away at what actually happened. Not that size is the only measure of health, but it's worth admitting that I had no faith that God could do anything "large" in such a "small" town. That said, this book is written out of both a burden and a hope.

This burden I feel comes from traveling around and seeing countless small towns that are on no one's priority list. In fact, even driving across America on our way from California to North Carolina, you cannot help but be overwhelmed by the massive amount of wide-open country with sparse communities everywhere. America is indeed a nation full of small towns.

But this is not just something I've seen in America. I have personally witnessed this same dilemma in my many trips to help churches in England. I meet people from Europe, Africa and Australia who tell me the same. This all leads me to believe it is more of a world problem than a purely American one. It's a problem that affects Christians everywhere if we are to take Jesus' commission seriously. Around the world, it seems that the cities have been prioritized with the gospel while the small towns have been left behind.

It's not all bad news. The hope that leads me to write stems from the lived experience that Jesus can and will make a substantial impact in small towns. It happened to us and I continue to meet other pastors who have the same stories of massive impact in small towns. It happens because God loves cities and small towns and Jesus is building his church in both.

My quest is not to eradicate mission in the cities but rather to help move toward a more biblical approach to viewing our mission. By more biblical, I mean it is a view that includes cities and small towns. I want to explore how we got to where we are, what Jesus actually did, and how we can learn from him to recalibrate our thinking so that we can advance the gospel everywhere.

What Specific Problems Do We Have?

The general problem that we have is that we see the small towns as irrelevant. But there are more specific problems that have led to this. The three most glaring problems that I think we have are as follows.

We have a theological problem. We don't see the call of God for us to go to small towns like we see it for large cities. The only way to fix the problem of not seeing small towns as important or ministry to them as necessary is to dive into the bible to see for ourselves what it has to say about them which is what we will address in chapter two.

Secondly, we have a sociological problem. We simply do not understand the current condition of small towns. Without even realizing it, I believe we have used Reaganomics, also known as, "Trickle Down Economic Theory," as our plan for successfully reaching America. We are assuming that if we impact the rich cities, the result will be a "trickle down" effect on the poor small towns.

There are a couple of reasons that I think this is an unhelpful way to think. For one thing, it is highly debated as to whether or not Reaganomics is actually true. It seems to me like a massive gamble when we are talking about getting starving people the bread of life. I don't think anyone, upon considering this seriously, would want to hope for the best.

Also, this premise is unhelpful. Simply put, it is cruel. It makes about as much missional sense as assuming because someone can pick up "Christian television" in a remote, unreached part of the world, they are fine.

You might think that's an unfair comparison. Unreached? Surely the small towns aren't equivalent to unreached people groups. Maybe they're not. But we are dead wrong if we think small town America, or small towns anywhere, have all been effectively reached for Jesus.

To prove that, in chapter three I want to talk about the current state of small- town America and expose the real need for the gospel there and, subsequently, small towns all over the world.

Thirdly, we have a philosophical problem. I mean we have wrong thinking and our thinking will have to change. As with any problem, we can have all the theological knowledge and sociological data, but we need our minds renewed to actually change. I hope in chapter four to help us see some of the detrimental mindsets driving the current mentality that small towns are irrelevant and unimportant.

Part One of this book is dedicated to helping us understand the problems we have that keep us from effectively engaging small towns in gospel ministry. If after these four chapters you are not convinced, read no further. However, my hope is that you will be freshly convicted by the life and ministry of Jesus, moved by the staggering need and compelled to be part of the solution. But that's only the beginning.

Part Two will flesh out practical methods for those currently living and ministering in small towns as well as for those thinking about going to small towns. Additionally, I will address how Christians and leaders in large city churches can really help as well and present the dream for us partnering together in this great work of advancing the gospel.

Admittedly I am an optimist, which makes me full of hope that in our generation we can see the pendulum shift back to a more appropriate view of mission to both cities and small towns so that Jesus can be glorified everywhere.

CHAPTER TWO

"JESUS OF NAZARETH"

Most of us have heard this title of Jesus before, but have you ever thought what Jesus of Nazareth actually means?

Those of us who read our bibles and go to church are in danger of hearing about Jesus so much we can easily forget to consider the significance of what we hear. We call this "inoculation." We are given so many doses of the gospel that it begins to lose its effect on us because we forget our real, ongoing need of it.

As Christians, we are meant to love and follow Jesus, however we probably know more about where our favorite athlete went to college and where good coffee comes from than where Nazareth was and what Nazareth was like. Additionally, many people called Jesus many things but what we learn as we explore those titles is that all of them are dynamic and life changing.

For instance, the bible tells us that Jesus is our "redeemer." We say this so often that we miss what we are saying. It has become cliché. When we dive into the meaning of the word, seeing that we were literally "bought with a price," we are brought to our knees in thankfulness and compelled again to shout the goodness of God from the rooftops.

In the same way, each title of Jesus is so powerful and all of the titles given to him weave together to bring us a full and awe-inspiring description of him.

So, what does Jesus of Nazareth mean? Who called Jesus by this name? Why did they call him that? What are we missing by not really grasping this description of Jesus? Let's have a look at some of those questions and see what happens to our hearts as we give ourselves to thoughtfully considering "Jesus of Nazareth."

Jesus Came From A Small Town

Literally, "Jesus of Nazareth" means, "Jesus from Nazareth." It isn't rocket science, and it is something most of us already know.

Jesus, Scripture tells us, was actually born and raised in two small towns. Bethlehem, where Jesus was born, had approximately 300 to 1,000 people and Nazareth, where Jesus was raised, had approximately 500 people living in it. Those are really small towns even by today's standards.

What else? Well, far from people viewing Jesus' earthly small town roots as acceptable or advantageous, it seems as though it was just one more thing that led to people hating or misunderstanding him.

The disdain of the small town seems to have been alive and well even when the bible was being written. Listen to this Old Testament prophesy about Jesus' birthplace:

> But you, O Bethlehem Ephrathah, who are too
> little to be among the clans of Judah, from you
> shall come forth for me one who is to be ruler in
> Israel, whose coming forth is from of old, from

ancient days.

– Micah 5:2

Micah is saying that Bethlehem, where Jesus was born, was so small it wasn't really worthy of even being one of the clans of Judah. The irony that Micah puts forth is how the most important person to ever live will come from a town that is considered irrelevant by mainstream society based in larger cities.

What Was Nazareth Like?

In addition to Jesus being born in a small town, Jesus was raised and lived the vast majority of his earthly life in the tiny town of Nazareth. Nazareth's culture and the significance of Jesus being from there is something that is misunderstood by most Christians today, according to commentator R.T. France:

Modern readers of the New Testament know
little about the geopolitical world of first-century
Palestine...

France goes on to describe how the southern province had racial, geographic, political, financial, cultural, linguistic and religious reasons to disregard Jesus of Nazareth. When we start to understand this, we can see why there was so much hostility around his continual announcement that he was God.

> The result is that even an impeccably Jewish Galilean in first-century Jerusalem was not among his own people; he was as much a foreigner as an Irishman in London or a Texan in New York. His accent would immediately mark him out as "not one of us," and all the communal prejudice of the supposedly superior culture of the capital city would stand against his claim to be heard even as a prophet, let alone as the "Messiah," a title which, as everyone knew, belonged to Judea (John 7:40-42)...*To read Matthew in blissful ignorance of first-century Palestinian sociopolitics is to miss his point. This is the story of Jesus of Nazareth.*
>
> - R.T. France

Did you know all of this about Nazareth? What does that change about your understanding of Jesus? It at least adds to our adoration of this, "man of sorrows." Additionally, if our birthplaces and dwelling places are predetermined by God (Acts 17:26), what does this tell us about God who chose to have Jesus born and raised in such a rejected place?

A legitimate question is, "Why was Jesus not born and raised in Jerusalem?" If the goal was widespread acceptance and influence that would seemingly make a lot more sense. In fact, I bet some of you reading couldn't imagine living 30 out of 33 years in such a remote and backwoods place as Nazareth. But that's exactly what Jesus did.

Who Called Jesus By This Name?

Right away, at the beginning of Jesus' earthly ministry, we can see that Jesus being from Nazareth would be one of the ways people would seek to discredit his authority. We can also see this by the various people and instances where this title was used, like in John 1:43-46:

The next day Jesus decided to go to Galilee. He

found Philip and said to him, "Follow me." Now Philip was from Bethsaida, the city of Andrew and Peter. Philip found Nathanael and said to him, "We have found him of whom Moses in the Law and also the prophets wrote, Jesus of Nazareth, the son of Joseph." Nathanael said to him, "Can anything good come out of Nazareth?" Philip said to him, "Come and see".

This is the first instance of someone seen participating in the disregard of Jesus because of where he was from. It comes right at the beginning of Jesus' earthly ministry.

Nathanael was from Bethsaida, a walled city that had been elevated by Herod as a Greek city-state giving it prominence in Galilee. Nazareth, on the other hand was a tiny, poor, country village. Nathanael, a city boy, hears that the Messiah whom the entire Old Testament is anticipating has come from the backwoods country village of Nazareth. He responds like he's just heard a great joke. It's laughable. "Nazareth! Can anything good come out of Nazareth?"

If Jesus was ministering in our day, claiming to be from the middle of nowhere, we would probably hire a public relations expert to come alongside of him and advise him to change the title, "Jesus of Nazareth" to something more exciting. In fact, it is not far off from what we have done. We have conveniently forgotten the humble town of Jesus' upbringing.

Who else used this description of Jesus? Many of the places where Jesus is called this are equally full of hostility and controversy. Consider the following examples.

This is the description that Pilate used to put on the cross above Jesus' head as crowds shouted and mocked (John 19:19). The sign was meant to read like a great joke, "Jesus of Nazareth, King of the Jews." What an oxymoron! Why would a king come from such a tiny town and why would a king die on a cross?

Jesus of Nazareth was the title the servant girl used when she accused Peter of being with him before His arrest (Matthew 26:71). Later Peter, who had originally denied knowing Jesus of Nazareth, used this description when he told the crowds at Pentecost the gospel (Acts 2:22), when he called to the cripple to stand and walk (Acts 3:6), when he stood before the Sadducees (Acts 4:10) and when he first preached the gospel to the Gentiles at Cornelius' house (Acts

10:38). Peter lost any embarrassment of being associated with Jesus of Nazareth and now used this title as often as he could to describe our Lord.

We may be embarrassed that Jesus, our Savior and King, is from "no-where-ville," but Jesus, it seems, was quite happy with this description of himself that was mostly used by demons and those who hated him. One of my favorite instances of this title being used is when Jesus trumped the brilliant and powerful Saul of Tarsus.

"Jesus of Nazareth versus Saul of Tarsus." Much like the story of David fighting Goliath, this is not the sort of match up that would lead people to put their money on Jesus.

Tarsus was a massive city in Paul's day. It's believed that the population was over 250,000. People came from all over to work in this very prosperous city known throughout all of the Roman Empire.

Maybe for this reason, when Paul was on trial, he referred to himself as being from Tarsus (Acts 21:39, 22:3). This would have immediately brought a sense of credibility to him. In other words, he wasn't some redneck. He was from a happening place.

Tarsus was rich with power and culture. There would

have been plenty of competition for every good opportunity. In other words, to make it from Tarsus, you really had to be something special. And Paul had made it. So Paul was special.

But Paul, who describes himself from such a noble place of birth, moments later tells how he was conquered by Jesus of Nazareth in Acts 22:8:

> And I answered, 'Who are you, Lord?' And he said to me, 'I am Jesus of Nazareth, whom you are persecuting.

This was a key part of Paul's testimony. I believe this was an integral part of God's work to humble Paul right from the start. Being knocked off your feet by a bright light in front of your friends is bad enough. But it probably would have been easier to swallow if the voice had said, "I'm Jesus of Rome" rather than Nazareth. At least Rome was powerful and respected. Getting taken down by someone from such a small and disrespected place is humbling in the same way that if a small girl beat me up I would be tempted to lie and tell people it was a cage fighter.

But Paul doesn't omit the facts of who conquered him. In Acts 9 when we first read of Paul's conversion, this is what we are told Jesus says in Acts 9:3-5:

> Now as he went on his way, he approached Damascus, and suddenly a light from heaven flashed around him. And falling to the ground he heard a voice saying to him, "Saul, Saul, why are you persecuting me?" And he said, "Who are you, Lord?" And he said, "I am Jesus, whom you are persecuting.

What's the difference in these two accounts? Paul chooses to elaborate some additional information in his Acts 22 account of this life-changing event. Paul adds that Jesus called himself, "Jesus of Nazareth" when he confronted Paul.

What I want you to see is that Jesus wasn't ashamed of essentially being, "Jesus the redneck from Nazareth". Why then are so many pastors and church planters reluctant to take ministry in small towns seriously?

This is the only recorded instance that Jesus used this title to describe himself. The only other place where Jesus acknowledges that he is Jesus of Nazareth is when the soldiers come to arrest him in John 18:3-8:

> So Judas, having procured a band of soldiers
> and some officers from the chief priests and the
> Pharisees, went there with lanterns and torches
> and weapons. Then Jesus, knowing all that would
> happen to him, came forward and said to them,
> "Whom do you seek?" They answered him,
> "Jesus of Nazareth." Jesus said to them, "I am
> he." Judas, who betrayed him, was standing with
> them. When Jesus said to them, "I am he," they
> drew back and fell to the ground. So he asked
> them again, "Whom do you seek?" And they said,
> "Jesus of Nazareth." Jesus answered, "I told you
> that I am he. So, if you seek me, let these men go.

Judas rallies some of the local police and they charge out in the night like a posse chasing a wild villain. When they announce who they are looking for, Jesus immediately identifies himself as the man they are seeking.

Interestingly, upon confronting Jesus from Nazareth, they too, like Paul, end up knocked off their feet. Isn't that amazing? The police coming in the night with weapons would have been intimidating. Being confronted by Saul of Tarsus, the brilliant and bloodthirsty enemy of the church would have been intimidating. However, in these only two accounts where Jesus uses this description of himself, his wannabe persecutors end up flat on their backs in submission to him.

There is something powerful about all the titles of Jesus. This title, Jesus of Nazareth, is no different. The fact that our Savior and Lord came from such humble beginnings and that this incited such a mixture of affection and animosity should make us all the more excited to understand it. But while many Christians would say they do, clearly the attitude many Christians have towards small towns show that we don't.

Simply put, Jesus was from a small town, so for Christians to not love small towns is, at the very least, concerning. Would we, if we had been born in Jerusalem, have even been ashamed to associate with the Savior of the world because of his weird accent, his odd clothes or his funny mannerisms? If not, why do we seem to hesitate to take people from similar places seriously today?

Jesus Ministered In Small Towns

Jesus wasn't just from a small town. Jesus ministered in small towns too. He wasn't like so many people I know who cannot wait to get out of a small town and move to a more happening place.

There are many movies dedicated to this theme. The nobody from nowhere moves away and becomes somebody from somewhere, only to be confronted by their past at some wedding where their big city friends inevitably meet "Cousin Leroy."

But Jesus didn't grow up in a small town and get out as soon as possible. Jesus lived most of his life in a small town and, once his ministry began, wanted to continually go to small towns even after his fame began to spread everywhere.

That's counterintuitive as well to us. Think about the Clampetts, that beloved backwoods family known as the "Beverly Hillbillies." Some of you might remember the song, which told the tale of how these poor dummies from the sticks struck oil in their yard and were quickly advised by their kinfolk to, "move away from there. They said, 'California is the place you oughta be. So they loaded up the truck and they moved to Beverly Hills that is. Swimming pools. Movie stars." No one questions the logic. You have the money now, why not live where everything's happening?

But Jesus didn't get famous and then quickly set up shop exclusively in a major city. Was Jesus clueless? Was he wrong? Or are we too quick to assume that's what we should do as Christians?

We spend a lot of time these days looking at what Paul did when it comes to church planting. Rightfully so. The guy was a beast. He was like Jason Bourne, Yoda and Braveheart combined. He was strategic, brilliant and effective. What could possibly be wrong with emulating Paul's approach to church planting? Nothing per se, however we are wise to remember that while church planting is a particularly post-resurrection activity, breaking open new and hostile territory with the Good News and seeing lives and culture transformed was something that we see firstly in Jesus' earthly ministry.

While we must learn all that we can from Paul, we

must not neglect Jesus' approach to ministry, which clearly included prioritizing small towns.

Isn't that what Paul is trying to communicate to the Corinthians where he explains that, while he plays a crucial role in their Christianity, he himself is not Jesus? He didn't die on a cross for them (1 Corinthians 1:13).

Of course the persistence and the cultural intelligence of Paul should be massive tools in our toolbox wherever we go. But we must also have a look at Jesus' earthly ministry before we start drawing hard lines as to where Christians should and should not be going with the gospel, which is where I fear we have veered off course.

The question is, "Did Jesus only go to large cities? Did Jesus go to small towns?" The actual fact is that Jesus went to both cities and small towns. Not one or the other. While it seems that Paul prioritized large, urban centers as his base of operations, Jesus used small towns too. Look at the following two verses:

> And Jesus went throughout all the cities and villages, teaching in their synagogues and proclaiming the gospel of the kingdom and healing every

disease and every affliction.

— Matthew 9:35

He went on his way through towns and villages,

teaching and journeying toward Jerusalem.

— Luke 13:22

Two Greek words are being used in these passages, "polis" which meant a city or town, and, "komas" which meant villages. What are the differences in these two destinations? A city was a town of greater or lesser size, with walls. A village was a country town, usually without walls.

It seems as though in Jesus' day what made your town important and identified it as the place to be wasn't how many fancy restaurants it had but was based on whether or not it had a wall around your area of dwelling.

At first glance this seems a little silly, but we do the same thing. We like the idea of living in a gated community because it elicits some sense of safety and prestige.

It was even truer in Jesus' day. Life was not civilized, as we know it. Tolerance wasn't the value that it has become in Western society. So having a wall to protect you from everyone else was something that many didn't want to live without. This made the small towns more vulnerable to attack and less desirable to live in.

However, what's interesting here is not the type of distinctions used between cities and small towns. What is truly amazing is that Jesus went and did the same teaching and miracles in both cities and villages. Jesus seemingly showed no deference to the cities over the small towns despite their significance.

Let me make this as clear as possible. Jesus didn't go to the largest cities and hope that his gospel and its powerful, life-changing works would trickle downstream to the small villages. Jesus went to both.

Jesus only had three years of earthly ministry before the cross. That's not a long time. In that incredibly short time span, Jesus chose to spend at least some of his precious time ministering into small towns.

Doesn't that mess with our paradigm just a little bit when it comes to where we place our priorities nowadays? I sincerely hope it does.

Let me press further. Ironically, it seems as if Jesus might have avoided some of the most major cities altogether in his earthly ministry.

> We should not be surprised that Jesus in an-
> nouncing [the gospel] kept on the move, going
> from village to village and, so far as we can tell,
> staying away from Sepphoris and Tiberias, the
> two largest cities in Galilee. He was not so much
> like a wandering preacher preaching sermons, or a
> wandering philosopher offering maxims, as like a
> politician gathering support for a new and highly
> risky movement.
>
> – N.T. Wright

Sepphoris and Tiberias were the major cities where we, if we were alive during that time, would have imagined Jesus going, but as far as we know, he didn't. He may have, but we simply don't know.

What the Scriptures clearly portray is Jesus, who we say we follow, ministering the same gospel in the same way to both people in cities and people in small villages. Addition-ally, Jesus didn't just visit the small towns, he felt obligated to preach to them.

"But he said to them, "I must preach the good news of the kingdom of God to the other towns as well; for I was sent for this purpose."

— Luke 4:43

The context and language here tells how important preaching to the towns was to Jesus. He leaves crowds of people begging him for healing and deliverance. His rationale for why he leaves is that he "must" go to other small towns as well. This is obligatory language. Literally, it was necessary for him. He had to go to small towns too. Obligatory things are things we must do. We have no choice. We have to do them.

Jesus even adds that he "was sent for this purpose." What he is communicating is that he wasn't throwing the small towns a bone. This wasn't a publicity stunt. This isn't like when an American Idol winner does a parade in their small town to say thanks to all the "little people" that got them to where they are today.

Jesus actually saw ministering to them as part of the reason he had come to earth. In Luke 19:10, Jesus says that he came to seek and save the lost. The lost were not confined to the large cities or the small towns.

The lost he wanted to seek and save were in both small towns and large cities, and so he was in both. They still are.

Jesus Sent His Disciples To Small Towns

Right after Jesus ministers to the cities and small towns he turns and begins to pass on this obligatory mandate to his disciples.

They were not to be spectators while Jesus did all the work of the ministry. He was sending them in his authority and on his mission. But where did he send them?

On their first missionary journey, Jesus sends them to a specific audience that they will already be acquainted with- Jews. Additionally, he gives them very specific instructions and indicates where they are to go in Matthew 10:11a:

And whatever town or village you enter...

Jesus had gone and ministered to small towns and big cities and they were to go to both as well. They weren't to pick and choose. They weren't to come up with their own idea of where to start. They weren't to pick the places that had their favorite restaurants. They were to simply go.

Interesting how simple this plan was that Jesus had. But did it work? We hear that from these trips Jesus sent them on, they would return with joy, amazed that even the demons had listened to them when they used Jesus' name (Luke 10:17).

What was happening? The Good News and power of Jesus was being displayed and lives were being changed; lives in the cities and lives in the small towns. Everyone was having a chance to be impacted by Jesus.

In Matthew 9, Jesus also told them to pray that the Lord of the harvest would send workers into his harvest. This is significant, because Jesus was God and could have said whatever he wanted to about how to accomplish the mission of reaching the world.

Jesus could have said, "Pray that the Lord of the harvest sends workers into the large cities and hope that one day it will trickle down to the small villages and country towns…" Jesus could have said this, but Jesus didn't.

So why do we so happily agree with this line of

thought? Jesus sent them to both and told them to pray that God would continue to send workers to both.

Jesus went to both cities and small towns. Jesus prioritized ministry to both cities and small towns. Jesus specifically sent out His disciples to both cities and small towns. What do you think that means for us in our day? It seems that we are to simply go to both as well.

CHAPTER THREE

SMALL TOWNS, BIG MISSION

Americans love their superstars. It's never one team versus another team; it's always one star player versus another star player. In a similar way, we view states by the big, important cities that they may or may not have. That means when we think of states like New York, we immediately think about New York City. We might even venture on to assume things about New York State based on New York City. We might be shocked if we realized that much of New York State is actually small-town/rural. The attitudes and beliefs of many of these people might not compare in the slightest to people who live in Manhattan, for example. It's the same way in many other states and major cities in America.

In my country, we have minimized the number of people who we imagine living in small-town America and truly believe that the life of America is found primarily in the cities and, maybe, the suburbs.

However, we couldn't be farther from the truth. So, what is the truth? How many people live in small towns in America? Maybe a better question is how many people are we deciding to regard as irrelevant, out-of-the-way, and unimportant as we solely pursue urban intentionality? The number is staggering.

According to the US Census Bureau, in 2010, there were 16,307 towns in America under 25,000 people and the number of people living in these communities was 33.7 million. That's a lot of people.

Just how many people is 33.7 million? I assume that my audience is probably Christians and probably even some Christian leaders or pastors. I also assume you care in some way about people in other countries who need the gospel. With those assumptions in hand let me give you a comparison.

If we decided, like we essentially have with small-town America, that countries with less than 33.7 million people were "unimportant, out-of-the-way, or irrelevant" and therefore were unworthy of our intentionality or our best missionary efforts, which countries would not make the cut? What if we were to apply our current strategy of just focusing on places with more people in hopes that eventually the other countries would be reached with the gospel? To which countries would we be postponing evangelism?

The number of countries with less than 33.7 million people is astounding: Morocco, Afghanistan, Venezuela, Peru, Malaysia, Saudi Arabia, Uzbekistan, Nepal, Mozambique, Ghana, North Korea, Yemen, Australia, Madagascar, Cameroon, Angola, Syria, Romania, Sri Lanka, Cote d'Ivorie, Niger, Chile, Burkina Faso, Malawi, Netherlands, Kazakhstan, Ecuador, Guatemala, Mali, Cambodia, Zambia, Zimbabwe, Senegal, Chad, Rwanda, Guinea, South Sudan, Cuba, Belgium, Greece, Tunisia, Bolivia, Somalia, Czech Republic, Portugal, Benin, Dominican Republic, Burundi, Haiti, Hungary, Sweden, Azerbaijan, Serbia, United Arab Emirates, Belarus, Austria, Tajikistan, Honduras, Switzerland, Israel, Jordan, Papua New Guinea, Bulgaria, Togo, Paraguay, Laos, Eritrea, El Salvador, Libya, Sierra Leone, Nicaragua, Den-

mark, Kyrgyzstan, Singapore, Slovakia, Finland, Turkmeni-
stan, Norway, Lebanon, Costa Rica, Central African Republic, Ireland, Congo, New Zealand, State of Palestine, Liberia,
Georgia, Croatia, Mauritania, Oman, Panama and still 70
more nations that wouldn't be prioritized if 33.7 million was
the cut off for what we view as important.

Somewhere in that list I bet there was a nation that
holds some special place in your heart. Maybe you've always
prayed and supported missionaries there. Maybe you've
served as a missionary there in short or long term missions.
For me it is the same. I would be deeply offended if we decided, because their overall population did not exceed some
arbitrary number, to deem them unworthy of a relevant,
intentional gospel effort.

God rebuked Jonah (in Jonah 4:11) for not caring like
he did for the 120,000 residents of Nineveh who didn't know
him. I wonder how God really feels about our arrogant assumption that 33.7 million people in America are not the real
priority for Jesus' Church because where they live is considered little, not big.

Small-town America is actually huge and small towns
are everywhere. If those 16,307 towns were distributed equal-

ly across America, we would have a town of less than 25,000 people every 12 miles. Every 12 miles!

What about in England? Doesn't everyone simply live in London? How many towns would be disregarded if we decided to only pursue ones above 25,000 people? According to a 2011 census, there were 7,339 towns or cities in England. Only 411 of them are above 25,000 inhabitants. That means that, out of 7,339 towns or cities, 6,928 of them are not worthy of our serious consideration. I guess we are just to hope that eventually they will get whatever floats downstream from the gospel working in London.

Again, I say this knowing many friends who lead churches in London. I respect them so much and I'm so thankful for the work that God is doing there and have an appreciation for the scope of what they are called to do. But that can't be our strategy for reaching England & Wales. Just hope things go well in London. Can we honestly picture Jesus advocating this?

Frankly, it is shocking how much of the population we are content to leave behind with the modern emphasis we have put primarily on urban ministry. God wasn't happy for the Ninevites to live in religious ignorance. He sent his messenger with his message. How do we honestly assume the tens of millions in small towns across North America and the UK don't matter as much to him because they don't live in a large city?

I think this brings up another point of tension or possible disagreement. The Ninevites were ignorant idol worshippers and therefore cannot be compared to small towns in our day can they? Aren't all small towns already Christianized?

Small Towns Need Jesus Too

Another massive assumption has been made that the work of evangelism, especially in small towns, is finished. Is that true?

Consider the following story. Ben and Lois Franks, both in their mid-twenties, moved to the Rhondda Valley in Wales to plant Hope Church Rhondda. Maybe you're thinking, "Wales? Didn't they have massive revival? Aren't they already Christians?" Tragically, no.

The Rhondda Valley has a total population of 83,000 people and the small town where the Franks have planted the church only has 3,000 people. In spite of its small size, this area has massive struggles including the highest suicide rate in the UK and the highest teen pregnancy rate in the UK, probably in all of Western Europe.

"Well, luckily there are tons of Christians and churches that can help with all of this." Wrong again. Only 0.09% of the inhabitants of the Rhondda Valley go to any religious service more than ten times a year. That means out of the 83,000 inhabitants of this broken valley, only 750 would be remotely considered as churchgoers, let alone Christ followers.

When the Franks realized this, they were broken to the core and set out to go and make much of Jesus in the Rhondda Valley. They both come from fairly middle to upper middle class upbringings. Both have seriously respectable college degrees and both could really "be something" in a massive city somewhere. But they are laying down their lives and their rights to see broken, lost people meet Jesus. Sounds a little like what we are supposed to do if I'm reading my bible right.

The reason for the Franks' story is to bring to light how far off we are when we imagine small towns as simple or evangelized. Too many of us picture towns like Mayberry from the Andy Griffith show. Mayberry was a town of just over 5,000 people with good clean fun, a humorous auto repairman and great pies made by Aunt Bee. Everyone in Mayberry was basically cordial to one another and if trouble did arrive, Deputy Barney Fife was prepared for it with the one bullet he kept in his shirt pocket. Sure, from time to time, trouble would blow into town. But by the end of the episode it was on its way out again.

This show went for eight seasons through the 1960s and did much to reinforce in Americans the view that while the rest of the country was flocking to festivals like Woodstock, dealing with hallucinogens, war, racism and rampant sexuality, small-town America was still innocent, pure and very naïve. Do you still believe that? Do you think modern small towns are still much like Mayberry?

The Modern Mayberry

Modern small towns are far from innocent or naïve. In America, for instance, our small towns are marked with poverty, drug abuse, broken marriages and are hot spots for meth-labs and human trafficking.

Small town concerns

Mount Airy, North Carolina is the actual town that "Mayberry" was based on and currently has a population of 10,417. How safe is "Modern Mayberry?" Well, in 2007 Mount Airy had a crime rate that was almost double the national average. Most of those crimes were related to theft, burglary and assault. It's safe to say that Deputy Barney Fife would've needed a little more than one bullet in his pocket to police the Modern Mayberry.

Can you see what has happened? This is important. Small-town America has fallen apart. Maybe it's not directly because of our focus that has primarily been on urban centers. That's certainly debatable, but what is not debatable is that small towns are just as in need of great leaders and great churches as any big city is. Is this really a surprise to us who believe Jesus is the only hope for all people everywhere?

Is it only in the town of Mayberry that crime has increased in the wake of the church's shift away from seeing small towns as needing the gospel? Not according to the statistics.

"Eighth-graders in rural America are 104 percent likelier than those in urban centers to use amphetamines, including methamphetamines, and

50 percent likelier to use cocaine... Eighth-graders in rural areas also are 83 percent likelier to use crack cocaine, and 34 percent likelier to smoke marijuana than eighth-graders in urban centers... bluntly put, Meth has come to Main Street, along with other drugs, and with magnum force aimed at our children...We've long heard the warning, and we're trying to reach beyond the cities to the suburbs and rural areas to see the reach of drugs across America," Attorney General Janet Reno told the U.S. Conference of Mayors... "We have to look at a radius beyond the cities."
—CBS.com, Deseret News and The National Center on Addiction and Substance Abuse at Columbia University

Eighth-graders! How does this affect your heart as a Christian? It should break it wide open.

Small Towns Are Not Christianized

Sure, small-town America hosts plenty of church buildings

and even a fair amount of tent revivals if that is your cup of tea. But have they ever really heard the gospel?

I've had multiple people tell me that in their entire lives of going to church in the South they had never heard someone tell them that, "God loved them because he wanted to love them; not because of anything they did or could ever do." That's the gospel.

Small towns often have, if they have anything, an assumed gospel. Don Carson wisely says that, "One generation believes the gospel, the next generation assumes the gospel but the next generation denies the gospel." But, with the data so clearly showing sin as reigning in small towns, we have to question if they haven't moved past an assumed gospel to a full-blown denial of the gospel.

"Well it doesn't look like that when I drive through a small town. There are churches everywhere!" Please don't let the church buildings that populate the streets of small-town America, or small town England and Wales for that matter, lead to an assumption that the inhabitants have been reached with the gospel. In fact, less and less of the younger generation is even attending church let alone having their lives shaped by the gospel. Small towns need Jesus. They need his gospel.

Weirdos And Wannabes

Who are the people planting and leading churches in the small towns? Now, there are some amazing churches and pastors in small towns across America. However, the answer is often times worse than "no one." People will go and plant churches in small towns, but what kind of people and what kind of churches?

There have always been longstanding denominational churches that built a building and gathered people, largely, based on historical affiliation with that particular denomination. However, many of these churches are failing to attract the next generation of people who are not as captivated by tradition as previous generations were. These large buildings with steeples are permanent fixtures in the landscape of small-town America. Some of them are doing much to reengage culture with the gospel. Some of them seem to be waiting for their "chariot in the sky." I don't want to take time here to address them right now. Rather I want us to take a few minutes to consider some of the new initiatives that are being started all the time in small towns.

Think about the last time you drove through a small town and paid attention to the churches that lined its streets. If it's been a while I'd encourage you to do so again. What I'm guessing you'll find, outside of the longstanding denominational churches, is a strange combination of two main categories of new churches; Weirdos and Wannabes.

The Weirdos

These are the churches with the really screwed up theology. They boast a cult-like dedication to their leaders. At worst they teach you how to handle snakes. At best they update you each Sunday on conservative news and on the exact date when Jesus will be coming back.

These are not the types of churches you want your kids or neighbors to go to. You cringe if you find out an unsaved coworker has been invited to one of these. These churches are isolated and they like it that way. They don't want accountability or any connection to leadership that might be looking to see if what they are doing or saying is right or biblical.

no accountability ↓ isolated from world

Their marquees are bizarre and kooky. I can imagine Paul saying, "Your marquees do more harm than good." Those who drive by and don't know Jesus are expected to slam on the breaks under conviction as they read, "God answers knee mail," which is apparently an attempt to get us to pray instead of sending emails. Those who are not Christians are supposed to be cut to the heart as they read, "TGIF: Tithes go in first." Those confused about their sexuality are to read, "I kissed a girl and I liked it and then I went to hell" and finally be set free from any temptation they have towards the same sex.

Now, to be fair, even though the weirdos are a little crazy at least they are willing to go to small towns. In fact, they like small towns just fine. But they aren't the only new guys in town...

The Wannabes

Wannabes are the poor planters who dream of the urban, fancy espresso, skinny jeans world of the urban church planter. But, alas, they are stuck cutting their teeth on some small town until they do well enough to get a swing at something more significant. But they aren't happy about it and it's plain to see.

The design of their buildings, names of their churches, styles of ministry, etc., resemble no connection or understanding of their audience. And they, frankly, don't care. They're not ministering to who's in front of them now, but who will be there one day when they are exalted to a larger platform.

These wannabes litter the main roads of small town America. A couple of times each year they get to get out and fill the halls of large church planter conferences where they get to hobnob with all of their heroes and finally eat some food and drink some coffee worthy of their sophisticated palate.

What makes them better than the weirdos is that they may preach accurate truth but it's void of a sincere love for the place they are at and the people who live there. In this sense, they are just as guilty as the weirdos of Paul's charge to, "speak the truth in love" (Ephesians 4:15). They get the truth part right, but not the love.

Most of us have been trained to think of small towns as already reached or not worthy of prioritizing. Our wrong conclusions about these towns and many of the churches that are located in them has only resulted in less of them being impacted by Jesus. This is not something we can afford to continue dismissing.

CHAPTER FOUR

RE-THINKING OBJECTIONS TO SMALL TOWN MINISTRY

One of the most powerful and helpful insights into how to do ministry effectively is found in Paul's first letter to the Corinthians:

> For though I am free from all, I have made myself
> a servant to all, that I might win more of them.
> To the Jews I became as a Jew, in order to win
> Jews. To those under the law I became as one
> under the law (though not being myself under
> the law) that I might win those under the law. To
> those outside the law I became as one outside the

law (not being outside the law of God but under the law of Christ) that I might win those outside the law. To the weak I became weak, that I might win the weak. *I have become all things to all people,* that by all means I might save some. I do it all for the sake of the gospel, that I may share with them in its blessings.

- 1 Corinthians 9:19-23

Paul is describing the great lengths to which he has gone in ministry. He was a fanatical Jew who, after being saved by Jesus of Nazareth, found himself gallivanting all over the Gentile world making much of Jesus and the gospel.

What Paul is not advocating here is some liberal form of tolerance whereby he joins wholeheartedly in sinful practices so as not to rock the boat when around people who don't believe what he does. What he's talking about is making the goal of ministry to see people saved by Jesus. He is saying that he, a Jew of Jews, was willing to even be as "one outside the law" with the intention that those outside the law would be "won" for Christ.

What we see Paul so clearly willing to do here is key

to us changing this problem we have. The answer is not for us to swing the pendulum to where we expect big city church planters to act like small town church planters. Rather, the answer is found in us being willing to become whatever necessary wherever we find ourselves in order that as many as possible would be saved.

Our Thinking Has To Change

Conferences and books, which address ministry in urban centers, are seemingly everywhere. Every major Network or Denomination, which isn't drinking spiked kool-aid or predicting Jesus' return this year is throwing considerable resources into impacting our nation's largest cities. Bible college students listen to podcast after podcast, read and study with the dream that soon, they too will engage in city ministry. I dare say not many of them are salivating at the potential of slugging it out in a town that doesn't even have a Target, a Chipotle or a coffee shop that isn't Dunkin Donuts.

If you go to the world's biggest bookstore, Amazon, and search various topics, you find what people want to read about. I tried this in an attempt to learn how to do ministry in my context and the results were telling.

When I first searched for "Church Planting" on Amazon I got 8,338 results. Can we just pause a second and thank God for this? There was a time, not very long ago, when no one wanted to plant churches. The fact that it now warrants so many results on a book search is a testament to the real, gospel led change occurring in our culture.

What's even more amazing is that planting a church has gotten harder than ever, not easier. Church is less popular in America than it was 50 years ago. The perks that our country gives to those in ministry are slowly going away. And if that wasn't enough, the hostility towards Christians who choose to engage the culture, rather than roll over or run away, is growing day by day. So, for church planting to be something that we want to learn about or feel compelled to pursue is an absolute miracle of God.

My conclusion from this first Amazon search indicated church planting to be a massive priority for us. Again, that's awesome!

The first time I searched for "church planting city" I received 193 results. Only two months later I searched for this again and this time I was given 208 results. This too is incredible. If you were prayerfully considering planting a church in a large city, you would have close to 200 choices of books and resources at your disposal. Sure, a lot of them are probably outdated or unhelpful for some other reason, but there are certainly some of them that would be of assistance to you. It is clear that planting churches in cities is a priority for some of us.

Finally, and you can guess where this is going, I searched Amazon again for "church planting small town." I had received over 8,000 possible resources for church planting; maybe I could get some good help on planting a church in my specific context. Not so much.

The results were telling, but it wasn't telling me that what I was doing was of any value according to most. I got six results for my search. Six. Let that sink in for a moment.

Ok, beggars can't be choosers, so I started diving in on those six. Three of them are more than ten years old, which doesn't mean irrelevant, but certainly makes irrelevance a possibility considering one of them speaks of the internet like it could actually be a big deal some day. One is about ministry in Bolivia. One is about ministry in the Middle East. One is, strangely, about Skid Row street ministry in Los Angeles and another one is something no one should ever read for reasons that don't need to be mentioned here. There are a few more examples if you search using "rural" as the key word but those resources seem dedicated to a very specific part of the small town world that is dominated by agricultural problems.

Here's what I came away with regarding my searches on Amazon. If I was going to plant a church in my small town, I was probably going to have to figure it out all by myself. I was going to have to read the best books on church planting in general and the best on church planting in the city and then try to figure out how to plant a church in a small town. I'm guessing some of you reading this are in the same boat.

In fact, I can't help but imagine there are thousands of people in my same situation. As I've started receiving opportunities to speak on this subject, I've been met by people crying and expressing to me that this was the first time they have heard that ministry in a small town was legitimate or necessary. I've heard people confess that they live with disappointment and frustration because God has them in a small town, not a big, sexy city. I've had people tell me that their

76

town of 700 needs Jesus, but no good churches will ever get started there. How on earth did we get here?

Why Is Small Town Ministry Not A Priority?

What we believe shapes what we do. We cannot begin to act differently until we investigate our beliefs and make the appropriate changes. That said, there are some powerful mindsets that produce this perception of why small town ministry isn't a priority for Christians today. I want to take a few moments to address some of those, but I warn you, for some it may feel as though I'm shooting some proverbial sacred cows.

Mindset #1- "Cities impact the small towns, so let's just focus on the cities."

I've already alluded to this some, but I want to say that thankfully we have been richly reminded of God's call to plant churches in cities – the biggest and most intimidating of them. We have current, real life stories of church planters who have braved large, intimidating cities and survived. They have more than survived. Many of these churches are thriving and seeing heaps of people added to the Lord and their culture changing all around them by the power of the gospel. Praise God!

This is a bigger deal than we often realize. Not long ago, Americans harbored a hateful view of their cities. Even Thomas Jefferson said, "I view the great cities as pestilential to the morals, the health and the liberties of man." What's Jefferson saying? He's saying that cities are bad for America. They are bad for our health and bad for our morals.

Thank God that while many Americans were running from the cities in fear, many Christians ran to them with the gospel. But we slowly adopted a line of thinking that believed if the cities were impacted by the gospel then eventually the small towns would be too. That "trickle down" way of thinking isn't just wrong, it's cruel.

Imagine that I loved my older son in hopes that my younger son would eventually be loved as well. That sounds wrong because it is wrong. This isn't the way we should treat people. Everyone deserves a chance to be prioritized by the love of Jesus. Everyone deserves a chance to have a great church in his or her town, large or small.

I am extremely grateful for those who have planted

in urban areas and to say I've learned a tremendous amount from them is an understatement. However, what I cannot get excited about is the mindset that too often seems to go hand-in-hand with ministering to the cities. That is the mindset that cities are more important to God than small towns. That is the kind of thinking that I am writing against.

Mindset #2- "Cities have more people, so they need more churches."

Fair enough. Logically, the more people you have to reach, the more churches you need to reach them. I couldn't agree more. My small town of 9,200 people doesn't need as many churches as Dallas, Los Angeles, Seattle, New York City, or Miami.

So how can this mindset be unhelpful? Well, let me ask this question. How many great churches does my town need? Let's insert some of the helpful buzzwords that we are using these days to define a great church. How many culturally relevant, gospel-centered, missional, Spirit-empowered, elder-led, etc., churches does my small town need? I hope you would at least agree on one. Would one great church in my small town be too many? Absolutely not. That said, I live here and lead a church here and, even though there are some great churches in our town, we need as many as possible because no one church can reach everyone.

Out of the 68,000 plus people that live in my county, only 29,000 of them report having a designated church that they attend. That means that over half of the people in my county still need to know the power of the gospel through a great church.

I've been so reminded of this by my friend Jim Tomberlin who helps churches consider this "redemptive potential" that is all around them. It's easy to just think about the people coming on Sunday and forget the thousands who don't. Even here, we have a lot of work to do still.

Let's jump back to the need for at least one intentionally gospel-centered church in every small town. As I've stated, this problem is not just an American one, but what if we Americans made that our goal?

What if we decided to put one "great" church in every small town in America? Well, there are presently 16,307 towns in America that would be considered small towns.

There are another 4,000 towns with 23 million people in what is called "urban fringe" because of their proximity to a city with 50,000 people or more. We will leave out the urban fringe for now, but it is worth considering that additionally 23 million people are similarly affected by the way we are currently prioritizing church planting.

Let's just speculate on how long it will take to just reach the goal of one great church per small town. Keep in mind that the status quo doesn't even consider these as vital to the success of reaching our nation with the gospel, which considerably slows down our pace. Even if one great church in every small town were our only goal, it would take decades to achieve.

Ed Stetzer says in the April 2016 edition of Christianity Today:

> When it comes to evangelicals being urban-centric in their mission's focus, the thinking goes like this, "Reach cities, reach the world; reach the cities, influence culture. I fully believe in this strategy and actively support it. The only exhortation I would offer is not to be so urban focused that gospel church planting is suctioned out of smaller cities, towns, and communities. *There are*

still areas outside of major urban centers and their metro-
plexes that are in desperate need of new church plants and
church revitalizations.

I want you to feel the reality of our current trajectory. Something has to change in the way we view our mission focus if we are going to reach the world with the gospel.

Mindset #3- "I only have one life, and I want to make it really count."

Deeply ingrained in the heart of every Christian should be the desire to live life in a meaningful way. Rightfully, we should feel that our lives must be lived radically in response to what Jesus has done for us. We should want other lives to be impacted and culture to change around us. That is very godly thinking.

But Christians, because we are humans, are rarely content with godly thinking. We usually mix godly thinking with worldly thinking which creates a mess.

We want to make a big impact, which is good. So we jump to the conclusion that we will have to live in a big city to make a big impact. This is what I mean by worldly thinking. We subconsciously assume that God needs a head start, something to work with if He is really going to do something impressive. However, this goes against one of the things God is most proud of about himself: namely, His ability to create something out of nothing. In fact, the whole bible starts off with God doing just this:

> In the beginning, God created the heavens and
> the earth. The earth was without form and void,
> and darkness was over the face of the deep. And
> the Spirit of God was hovering over the face of
> the waters. And God said, "Let there be light,"
> and there was light.
> – Genesis 1:1-3

The Spirit of God hovers over darkness, formlessness and the void of the uncreated. God doesn't say, "There's nothing down there, let's go to another planet with more potential."

Our God is not intimidated or limited by the lack of resources he has to work with. He is the Creator and gets busy creating. He engages the uncreated with purpose and order. This is our God; the God who knows the end from the beginning; the God who is not limited; the God of the impossible, who says that nothing is too hard for him.

However, we often act like God needs something to work with and if something big is going to happen, we assume it will take a big start to get it going.

The God of the bible loves beating the odds because it shows us how powerful he really is. He creates the world out of nothing, whittles down Gideon's army so that he can get even more glory for the victory, brings Jesus out of an inconceivably small town and uses 120 Christians praying in a little room to spark a worldwide movement that we are all benefiting from today.

We too easily forget that God doesn't need a massive headstart to get going. If we want to make a big impact for Jesus, we only need to rest our faith in the bigness of him. I love how William Carey puts it, "Expect great things from God. Attempt great things for God."

In fact, arguably America's greatest theologian, Jonathan Edwards, went to minister to American Indians. In the same way, Martyn Lloyd-Jones, the famous Welsh preacher, left a brilliant future in medicine in London to return to pastor a church in a small town in Wales. Were Edwards and Lloyd-Jones alive today, we might consider their choices a waste. But they did not.

But that gets into our motives. If we have amazing examples, like Edwards and Lloyd-Jones, of gifted leaders who chose to use their lives to minister in remote places, why is it not good enough for us? Who do we really want to make an impact for? Could all three of these previous mindsets just as easily be a cover up for the following one? I think so.

Mindset #4 – "I secretly want a large church and a large profile and I know I won't get it if I plant a church in the middle of nowhere."

If that is you, I could prove to you the legitimacy of planting churches in small towns from the bible until I was blue in the face, but until I promise you social network popularity and speaking opportunities in large conference settings, you will remain just as uninterested. This is because many of our biggest objections to doing the right things come, not out of biblical misinterpretation, but out of looking out for our own personal interests.

Because this way of thinking is so detrimental, let me

be frank with you, you should go and repent. You should ask God to show you where and when ministry became about you and not him. You should go back to the bible and let it redefine what success really looks like. Friends, we must remember that ministry idolatry is subtle and dangerous. It's far easier than we think to start doing the work of ministry for all the wrong reasons.

That said, you know we could just let God decide the profile we get or don't get as ministers of the gospel. I know it seems a little old school, but we don't have to see every thought we've ever had about Jesus as a chance to gain more followers on social media outlets. We don't have to see the location of where we live and the size of our church as a stepping-stone to greater opportunities.

It's actually kind of sick when you stop and think about it. The point I'm trying to get at is that we are sinners and our sin really affects our motives.

In regards to small town church planting, I fear that this obsession with being a superstar pastor and having a massive following on Twitter can result in less churches being planted in areas that desperately need a great church. That is a problem.

Wanting to make our lives count and to make a difference is fine. But it's who we are trying to impress that matters. If we want a bunch of pastors and leaders to think we are awesome then, yes, we probably have to move to a big city. However, if the goal is for people's lives and our culture to be changed by Jesus, then we should know that this happens as easily in a small town as in a big city.

We need to be convicted again that Jesus still sends his disciples to both small towns and big cities because he is building his church all over the world. We need to know that there is a massive mission field in small towns. Finally, we need to adopt a more biblical mindset that compels us to stop dichotomizing and acting like the southern Judeans did towards the region where Jesus lived. We need to go with the gospel everywhere and do it with all of our hearts so that, "some might be saved," as Paul said in 1 Corinthians 9.

My desire is not that people will swing the pendulum back too far in the opposite direction towards small towns. How tragic would that be! Rather, we need a mature respect and love for each other. We need to each be where God has called us to be and resist the temptation to dichotomize or polarize. This is just another successful attempt of the enemy to divide and conquer Jesus' church.

A win for the city is a win for the small town. A win for the small town is a win for the city. Last time I checked "the field is the world" and "the earth is the Lord's" which means we are on the same team.

Be Where God's Called You To Be

Weirdos and Wannabes succeed in small towns because too many good planters are "too good" to waste their lives on what Jesus saw as valuable.

We need great churches planted in every small town. But this isn't for everyone. Consider this provocative quote by Jordan Grooms:

> If God's called you to be a king, don't stoop to be a missionary; but if God's called you to be a missionary, don't stoop to be a king.

For three years of my life I traveled and spoke on short-term missions. This was a quote that always bothered me in a very godly sort of way. I was so convicted about the lack of churches in the 10/40 Window and how many languages that had not yet heard the gospel that I felt as if anyone who wasn't packing their bags into coffins like the missionaries of the Student Volunteer Movement and going overseas was wasting their lives.

I also believed that Christians in churches in America should give all their money straight to para-church ministries like the one I worked for if they wanted to do anything that actually mattered. I assumed that the work in America was done and that if people didn't believe in Jesus by now, they had simply missed their opportunity. Looking back, that was a really unbalanced way to think. It was also very simplistic and, frankly, ignorant.

Now, the irony is that I am leading a church in America and trying to convince everyone I meet to be "on mission" right here in our small town. We still give money and send teams to countries like Nicaragua, Turkey, and Nepal and we are so thankful to be able to. But my perspective of where mission is needed has moved from only certain parts of the world, to the whole earth. Which is actually what Jesus said from the beginning (Matthew 24:14).

Thankfully, I also have the privilege of having many

of my best friends leading churches in large cities around the world including Singapore, Johannesburg, London, Philadelphia, Houston, Los Angeles, Raleigh, New York City, St. Louis, Perth and Oklahoma City. I thank God for those men and I can honestly say I feel we have a real mutual respect and love for each other and desperately want to see each other thrive.

There's no posturing because one guy's location is larger or another guy's church size is larger. Who cares? We are saved by grace and here for a short little time on earth where we get to live passionately for the sake of Jesus. The bible says our life is like a vapor. We should not waste time comparing ourselves by ourselves, which the bible says is unwise (2 Corinthians 10:12).

Great Christian leaders fall into the trap of assuming that what we are doing for Jesus is more important than what someone else is doing all the time. Let's just admit it, it's hard to be balanced when you are feeling the passion that real conviction brings.

I deal with this struggle as well. I find myself wanting to be critical of people not doing things exactly like I do them. But I don't want that to get the best of me. It would be easy for me to overstate this need for churches in small towns to make it sound like ministry everywhere else was illegitimate. But that would be unhelpful, simplistic and ignorant. We are all building the same wall together. One of us may be stationed at the Valley Gate, while another at the Dung Gate, but we are all building the same proverbial wall (Nehemiah 3:13-14).

Let me not give you the impression that conviction is bad. Far from being bad, conviction is what God uses to get us moving in the right direction. God makes people so convicted that they are hardheaded for his sake (Ezekiel 3:7-9).

It took some real hardheaded people to convince the mainstream culture, who had been dominated by Jeffersonian hatred towards the cities, that Jesus wanted to love those people too. It will take more hardheaded, convicted people to help bring the balance back where we see Jesus' mission everywhere and it will take a lot of maturity for us all to stand side by side for the gospel (Philippians 1:17).

My appeal is simply for a healthier perspective. One is not better than the other. Small is not better than big. Big is not better than small. In fact, a huge tragedy is that we are missing real opportunities to dialogue and learn from one another. What if we applied Grooms' quote to our modern view of church planting? What if we said:

> If God calls you to plant in the city, don't stoop
> for the small town; but if God calls you to the
> small town, don't stoop for the city.

Like Mellencamp alludes to in his song "Small Town", if God puts you in a small town, that should be good enough for you. If God puts you in a big town, that should be good enough for you. This puts the emphasis on where God calls us, not on our concepts about who and where is most important. To be honest, as subjective as that may sound, it is a lot safer than us picking which one is more valuable.

Historically, we have not been the best judges of where and who is more important. Tragically, it wasn't long ago in this country that our leaders thought it was more profitable to prioritize whites over those with color.

We have not been prioritizing cities long enough to know if it will lead to mass impact in small towns. But I don't think we are supposed to figure that out. And I certainly don't think we are supposed to wait and see; something we disciples fall into easily.

If you remember, right after Jesus' disciples are commissioned by him to go into all the world to be witnesses of the gospel, they are found standing and staring into heaven waiting to see what will happen next when two angels show up essentially saying, "Stop procrastinating...go do what he said" (Acts 1:6-11).

We are good at coming up with stalling techniques. We are not so good at hearing and obeying. Let's do what Jesus said. Let's go anywhere and everywhere and let's work together to see him glorified.

Part Two

HOW TO DO MINISTRY IN SMALL TOWNS

CHAPTER FIVE

UNDERSTANDING YOUR SMALL TOWN

Morehead City is located at the very bottom of an island chain called The Outer Banks that runs off the coast of North Carolina and up to the Virginia border. No, I'm not trying to make you jealous, but I am trying to set the stage for understanding where I live.

If you were going to plant a church in my town or in any of the island towns along our coastline, you probably would not want to go with a mountain themed name and facility because our closest mountains are hundreds of miles away.

I know that sounds very elementary, but I knew a guy

who didn't get it. He was a great guy, but he didn't get that this town, and the coastal towns like ours, derive their identity from salt water. He didn't like the sand, the salt water, going out in boats, etc. So, he didn't go to the beach or out in the boat. He designed his house to resemble a beautiful loft from some city he loved. He did not seem happy here and maybe he wasn't happy here. But what this resulted in amongst local folks was misunderstanding and probably some mistrust.

Those who call The Outer Banks home, minus a few folks who may have been reluctantly relocated because of occupation or military service, really love this place and the saltwater culture that surrounds it. They even have a term for people who were born and raised in and around the water here, "salty." Even folks who are relocated here often reluctantly end up seeing the light, buying a boat and sticking around!

It's extremely safe to say that "saltwater" is what makes our town tick. Living by the ocean provides us with abundant fresh seafood, a large shipping port, vibrant tourism and beachfront real estate that help to fuel our economy.

So, what does that have to do with ministry or church

planting? Everything. It was this knowledge that we used to decide the name of our church, the rhythms of our small groups, and even the style of each of our facilities. For example, we named our church One Harbor because everywhere you look there are harbors. This made it easy for me to point and say things like, "We want to be a safe place, a deep place, a place that is humble but effective."

To come in and attempt to do ministry in a way that ignores the love of saltwater or to fight against that would have been foolish. Culture is the context that we will plant the seed of the gospel into.

That's what makes my small town tick. Do you know what makes your small town tick? What is it that everyone loves? What do people rally around? What do they celebrate? What do they mourn? What fuels your economy? Take a moment to consider your answers to these questions.

If you don't know those answers, that's ok but you cannot remain in ignorance. Also, it's important to note that you don't get this information by searching Google or Wikipedia. You can only find this out by listening and watching people live their lives. To do that, you first have to really care. You have to care enough to do life with them.

Again, this is what we see the best missionary ever, Jesus, doing. He "reclined at the table" with people who were far from him in their hearts. That word "reclined" does not mean, "passed out tracts and left." We see Jesus being called the "friend" of sinners. Jesus doesn't protest this. He was their friend. He was their trusted confidant. We pastors can learn a lot from Jesus as a missionary.

The church planter I mentioned wasn't a bad man, but he missed out on some good opportunities. He could have pushed past his own preferences and joined in a boat trip or some time on the beach so that he could understand those in his town and they could begin to understand him.

If you don't know what your small town values, there is a high probability you are doing something intentionally or unintentionally that is leading people to misunderstand you or not trust you. Those are two feelings that we should never want people to have about us.

Contextualization Is About Clarity

What we are discussing here is the subject of contextualization. That is taking something foreign and fitting it into a context or culture. Most successful businesses know that contextualization is imperative. In fact, restaurants and businesses always fail when they act above their local clientele. When they offer a version of doing business that comes across as pretentious or condescending to the locals, they are doomed before they begin.

Sadly, many churches fail to make the same connection. They reach what they feel is a ceiling in church effectiveness that cannot be penetrated. It is not a real ceiling although its consequences are very real. This false ceiling is failing to penetrate culture with a contextualized approach to sharing the gospel and doing ministry.

But is this a biblical concern? I believe so. Listen to Paul describe his desire for clarity in his ministry:

> But we have renounced disgraceful, underhanded ways. We refuse to practice cunning or to tamper with God's word, but by the open statement of the truth we would commend ourselves to everyone's conscience in the sight of God.
>
> – 2 Corinthians 4:2

Paul wanted to put forth the truth plainly. He didn't want there to be any reason not to trust him. He wanted what they believed to be as clear as possible.

Now, this in no way guarantees that all people will like you. In fact, when you do clearly communicate your beliefs and intentions, those who have opposing views may even hate you for them. Paul's response to that is that the gospel is veiled to those who are perishing (2 Corinthians 4:5-6 ESV). Paul's goal in ministry is not to gain more social media followers and popularity. He is also aware that many people will reject Jesus regardless of how well he preaches or leads. Paul sees it as his responsibility to be so clear in the way he does ministry, that people are only left with two options: to reject Jesus or worship Jesus. My point is that I don't feel enough pastors in our day are as concerned as Paul was about this kind of clarity in their ministry.

Understanding Your Small Town Still Leads To Offense

Just because you properly understand your culture doesn't mean people will never get offended. On the contrary, Paul was run out of town multiple times precisely because of his ability to understand culture. If we are faithful to apply the gospel to the culture we find ourselves ministering in, people will be deeply offended.

The way you and I do ministry will at some point lead to offense, but why will people get offended? Will people be offended by the gospel or by something trivial? Again, I appeal to Paul's methodology expressed to the Corinthians:

> We put no obstacle in anyone's way, so that no
> fault may be found with our ministry...
> – 2 Corinthians 6:3

Is Paul advocating liberalism? Is Paul suggesting a hyper-seeker-sensitive version of ministry that will lead to no one being offended? Absolutely not! However, Paul is wisely ministering in a way that leads to people getting offended by the right things, not the wrong things.

Paul will clearly remind his readers in Rome what is the right thing to be offended about:

> ...They have stumbled over the stumbling stone,

as it is written, "Behold, I am laying in Zion a stone of stumbling, and a rock of offense; and whoever believes in him will not be put to shame.

- Romans 9:32b-33

I believe Paul sees the way we do ministry like clearing a path for people to come to the rock of offense, Jesus, and either worship or reject him. He goes out of his way to not personally be a stumbling block in his own life and character. He is also vehemently opposed to others doing things that could lead to people being offended prematurely.

To reject Paul personally or to misunderstand what he is doing and to walk away is, from Paul's perspective, a loss. To get to Jesus and then reject him because of the exclusivity of his claims, to see his teachings as too hard, or because the cost is too great is tragic, but acceptable.

The reason that I bring this up is because I don't believe some of us as church planters and pastors think like Paul. Or, we did when we first started out in ministry, but it's been way too long since we considered what we are doing in ministry and why we are doing it. This happens in all types of churches.

I had a very conservative church planter who loves to surf and is very casual tell me that he likes to really dress up on Sundays so that people will struggle with liking him. His logic was that he wanted to make it hard for people to like his church so that if they stayed it would literally be a miracle.

This pastor has some good intentions that have led to some very odd and unhelpful conclusions. He is intentionally adding obstacles before people ever even get to the real rock of offense, Jesus.

Contrast what this pastor is doing to Paul's personal testimony that we read earlier in 1 Corinthians 9 about the lengths he went to reach people. He was willing to "become" whatever it took to "all people".

Paul is on the other extreme from my friend who loves to surf but wants everyone to struggle with him personally before they meet Jesus. Paul saw himself as a slave to culture, not sinful culture, but to the various cultures he found himself in. He did not come in as the Paul whom he had always been. He came into various contexts with only one ambition, to do whatever it took for people to be saved.

On the other hand, I know some hyper-charismatic pastors who wear the fact that people view them as "weirdos" as a badge of honor. They seem to think that the Holy Spirit comes to freak everyone out instead of glorify Jesus, something for which I can find no scriptural evidence. Because of this, they celebrate when they should grieve the fact that unsaved townspeople leave confused.

Consider Paul's application of logic when he discusses with the Corinthians how to handle speaking in tongues:

> If, therefore, the whole church comes together and all speak in tongues, and outsiders or unbelievers enter, *will they not say that you are out of your minds?* But if all prophesy, and an unbeliever or outsider enters, he is convicted by all, he is called to account by all, the secrets of his heart are disclosed, *and so, falling on his face, he will worship God and declare that God is really among you.*
> -1 Corinthians 14:23-25

Paul was not trying to silence speaking in tongues or prophecy, on the contrary he was encouraging them to desire and excel in these gifts. However, Paul was not wanting them to miss that "unbelievers and outsiders" coming into their meetings were opportunities for clarity, not confusion, in hopes that conviction and repentance would come.

This example Paul gives is not purely hypothetical for my fellow charismatics. In Acts 2, speaking in tongues, albeit in known languages, proves to be a very confusing event for the onlookers not yet part of Jesus' church. They wrongly assume these people were crazy drunk early in the morning.

Peter and the rest of the folks in the early church don't start high-fiving each other for being "Jesus freaks." That's because thousands of people thinking they are weirdos is not a win. It's a loss. So what does Peter do? Peter jumps up and brings clarity and preaches the gospel and thousands get saved as a result. That's a win.

Avoiding Copy + Paste

In small towns, it is imperative that we do not import an unadjusted ministry methodology from an urban context into a small town context. I call this failure to contextualize "copy + paste." It is a seductive trap that too many church planters and pastors fall into. It goes like this: something works somewhere and so it must work here.

Pastors visit other churches, read books, go to conferences, etc. and look for the latest and greatest methodology that they can simply paste into their context. The problem is that more often than not this leads to Proverbs 13:12, "Hope deferred that makes the heart sick…" The paste doesn't work; the miraculous events that transpired "over there" didn't translate on the ground "here."

We have inherited this way of thinking from many non-missionary minded church planters in the last half-century that did exactly this. They wanted to make a difference in their city and they felt stuck. In some ways, it seems like it may have worked for many in the past. However, the world was different then in regards to globalization and their measures of success were often far different than ours today.

For example, thankfully many who plant churches now are not measuring success by the amount of people who attend on a Sunday alone, but by how the culture around us is being impacted by our intentional focus on loving and living out the gospel. That means not much can be easily "pasted" because every context is different.

The irony of all of this is that usually the guys who are being copied are themselves great missionaries to their culture. Tim Keller, the lead pastor of Redeemer Presbyterian in New York City, immediately comes to mind. Everywhere I go around the world, I can see people pretending to be Tim Keller and assuming their context is just like his.

It's understandable why this would be tempting. Keller is a cultural and missiological genius. But this is because, like other successful church planters, he has done the hard work of serving, learning and earning the right to be heard within his cultural context. However, tragically, most of the time it's the application that is adopted, not the painstaking process. That's because the application is far easier than the process.

The fact is that very few people are willing to do the hard work necessary to actually understand their culture and see it changed. So they settle for the quick-fix ministry equivalent of weight loss pills. In Keller's case, they just copy what he does and expect the same results, which won't happen. So they will end up more disappointed.

Reformatting Instead of Pasting

What the world needs is a new breed of church planters who

act like good missionaries by refusing to "copy + paste" anything except what is scripturally imperative. Instead we must painstakingly reformat everything that's methodological, looking for a way to apply it to our culture, or disregard it.

What I mean is that we can take the deep theological truths that a Keller, for example, provides very easily. However, the way of applying those truths should be pushed through a grid of culture and context. This is additionally made harder because of how selfishly we naturally view ministry.

The fact is that everyone has preferences to how ministry should be done. Some of these preferences are just personal and concern issues that are open handed (i.e. music style, amount of media, dress code, style of preaching, design of facility, rhythms of small groups, etc.). But to really be missionaries, we have to abandon our personal preferences for the sake of gospel advancement.

Think of it like a French fry processer with a wire grid that a potato is shoved through, turning it into French fries on the other side. Our views of what we want to do are the potato. The things we learn about the culture we are trying to reach is the wire grid. We must push our views of these things that are open handed issues through a contextual grid. Only then can we successfully engage our culture.

Now, not everyone has done this with issues that are open handed. That is, issues that we can change without being outside of Christian Orthodoxy. Some church planters, in an effort to engage culture have changed the wrong things; the close handed issues. Things like inerrancy of scripture, for example, are closed handed. We don't get the right to change those things. But we can intentionally work to explain those topics to people outside of Christianity.

What I want to do, as you consider culture, is help you remember that some things cannot and should not change. But a lot of things can change. And fewer things are closed handed then we think.

Now, as mentioned already, this takes on another dynamic if a church planter actually starts to do this well. It seems to be a temptation almost impossible to resist to turn around and market the applications of the process to desperate hopefuls who aren't seeing the results they long for and are willing to try anything.

To paraphrase an ancient Asian proverb, we too often give people fish rather than teach them to fish. Much like that analogy, the church planters who adopt our application too quickly return home only to sadly watch the dream of successful ministry flounder on the deck and eventually die like every previous attempt before.

We who, by the grace of God, manage to engage our culture successfully must avoid enabling another generation of "copy + paste" pastors. We must, to the best of our ability, force those who would ask us for help into a reformat mode. We must ask questions to make them think, rather than give them all the answers. We must refuse to give them the proverbial fish in our hands when they ask for it. Rather we should put a rod in their hands and teach them to fish for themselves.

If You Build It...They May Not Come

In a big city, you can rightly assume that there will be some number of people who would right away agree with you and your style of ministry. This is not always true in small towns.

An example of this is when Hillsong started a church in Manhattan and had thousands on their opening Sunday. Within four years they now have 7,000 weekly attendees.

What we see is that there was already an audience that wanted what a Hillsong Church would bring; quite a large audience in fact.

However, smaller contexts, by their very definition, are small and therefore do not benefit from the large contingencies of people that might identify immediately with your vision for ministry like an urban setting would. It would be highly unlikely that in my town of 9,062 people that we would draw over 7,000 people in four years.

There's a famous line from the 1989 film, "Field Of Dreams" where Kevin Costner's character is told, "If you build it they will come." He later realizes that he is meant to build a baseball field in his backyard so that ghosts of legendary baseball players can have a place to play again. He is guaranteed results if he just builds this field. The same is not necessarily true for you and I as church planters in small towns.

There may not be a ton of people just waiting for you to start that church that you dream of. To reach the people of a small town, much work must be done to ensure people rightly understand who you are and what you are doing.

These lessons are important for all church planters,

but are far more evident for church planting in small towns. The simple fact is that the smaller the context you are working in, the smaller the margin for error.

If you totally misread your culture in a large city, you may only reach a handful of people who already agree with you and are willing to travel to be part of your church. If you totally misread the culture of a small town, you may not reach anyone. You may only attract people who have been kicked out of all the other churches before you arrived.

If this all comes as news to you, don't be overwhelmed. But let this be an encouragement to you to become intentional in your efforts to understand the context that Jesus has put you in. Don't assume anything about the culture. Spend time in the community with people who don't go to your church already. Settle in for the long journey of becoming a good missionary. Then, ask tons of questions. Listen to the music they love. Find out what they love. Find out what they celebrate. Find out what they mourn. Find out what they worship already. Look for ways to become "all things" to them so that "some might be saved."

Chapter Five Pop Quiz: How Well Do You Understand Your Small Town?

I hope none of this is discouraging in a way that is paralyzing. Figuring out what makes your small town tick takes time. Use the following questions to see how you are doing and to help you think of additional questions you should be asking yourself.

1. What do the annual festivals that your small town hosts tell you about what they value? Does what your town celebrates have any redeemable qualities that show how God has prepared them for the gospel? (Think of Paul's visit to the Areopagus in Acts 17. The culture of worship was redeemable, but the objects of worship were not.)

2. What do people in your small town fear the most? How does the gospel apply to that?

3. In a small town, usually the largest gathering of people is at a high school football game or at a graduation ceremony. How many people attend these events, or similar events in

your small town?

4. At these large events, attendees typically come with no expectation of building relationships. That said, what is the largest size crowd that folks in your town regularly gather in where they would have a hope of meeting others? What does that tell you about the size of the main gathering space you should have at your church if you want people to not automatically feel overwhelmed or disengaged?

5. The gospel message is already extremely foreign, the question is, is your facility helping or hurting you reach people who are not yet Christian? What do the most popular restaurants, bars or other main gathering spaces in your town look like? Have you ever been in them and considered this? If not, visit the most popular watering holes and think intentionally. What colors and materials are being used primarily? Now ask yourself if your church facility also uses any of these colors and materials or would your facility look and feel very foreign to folks in your town who don't already attend a church?

6. In small towns, the blessing and curse is that everyone

seems to know everyone. Are you using this to your advantage? When you are out in the community, do you choose to go to the same places over and over so that you can build relationships with people? Have you ever even considered this? Do you go to the grocery store and coffee shop just for groceries and coffee? If so, what opportunities are you missing to engage your small town? Remember that Jesus and his disciples showed up in a town where Jesus gets water and his disciples are sent for food. They return with food and Jesus has impacted a women's life so significantly that the entire town begs Jesus to stay and teach them too. Intentionality makes all the difference.

7. What style of music do most of the folks in your town like? Have you ever considered shaping the style of your singing on Sundays to reflect this at all? Many pastors never even think about this. We listen to Christian radio and pick songs that we like and play them exactly how they are played to already Christian audiences. What could you do to change the style of your music to reflect the culture around you? For instance, one of our site locations, Beaufort, has a love for folk music so we chose to use a banjo, a mandolin and folky

singing for the style of music. The message of the songs is still the same, but the style better reflects the style of music the culture loves. Can you reformat that example to fit your own context?

8. Church names often become the sacred cow of the church unnecessarily. Jesus died for his church, not our church names. The problem is that we often pick names that make no attempt to communicate to people outside the church. There is a popular radio show in our area where one of the characters plays the very opinionated, "Reverend Billy Ray Collins" and the name of his church is, "Sword of Joshua Independent Full-Gospel Pentecostal Assembly." Most people in our area can quote that entire church name and they all know why it's funny. It's funny because so many churches are named crazy things that no one outside of their church understands. Now, I bet you feel a little better about your church's name after hearing the one above, but don't miss the opportunity to ask yourself if your church name makes sense to people who don't know Jesus? Are you unintentionally sending a message from the very beginning with insider language that makes people on the outside not feel welcome?

If so, would you be willing to consider changing your church name to something that outsiders could immediately relate to?

CHAPTER SIX

OVERCOMING SMALL TOWN MINDSETS

As mentioned in the beginning of this book, most of us know that how we think determines what we do. This is no different for folks in small towns. A lot of tradition and history is behind their actions and this cannot and should not be ignored.

It's important to remember that there are always redeemable and unredeemable mindsets that exist. Redeemable mindsets are ones that are not in conflict with how the bible teaches to live. Unredeemable mindsets are those that are opposed to living in a way that honors God. If we really seek to change the aspects of the culture that are not in line with the gospel, we have to learn how to address the mindsets that produce those actions, not just the actions themselves. Paul clearly articulates this in Romans 12:2:

> Do not be conformed to this world, but be
> transformed by the renewal of your mind, that by
> testing you may discern what is the will of God,
> what is good and acceptable and perfect.

We need our mindsets renewed before we can begin to live out God's perfect will. In the same way, understanding the ways that small town people think is at the core of knowing how to better point them to Jesus. Do all people in all small towns think alike? Is it that simple? No, it's not.

However, there are some basic mindsets that seem to be prevalent in most small towns. As we discuss those, think of which ones are present in your town and of additional ones I haven't mentioned that exist where you live.

Mindset #1: Small Town Folks Like Saying They Are "From Here"

This is one of the first things people from a small town bring up when they are introducing themselves (I've already done it today while getting my teeth cleaned and feeling insecure about my lack of flossing.). They also like to point out, "You aren't from around here are you?" to people who clearly seem to not fit in.

In my town, we can tell when people aren't from here by their "Yankee accent," their shiny boat clothes that have never actually encountered salt water, etc. What needs to be said is that often times small town residents derive a very strong sense of their identity from being "born and raised" in the town they are living in.

I am not immune to this. I have a series of tattoos on my arm commemorating my heritage here in North Carolina. I have a North Carolina flag with our state's motto, our Carteret County seal, a blue crab because I'm from a part of Morehead known as Crab Point and the words, "Born And Bred" inscribed underneath all of the above. It goes without saying that I'm proud of where I'm from, and when I debated about what to get a tattoo of, it was super easy to go with a theme that showed homage to my hometown.

Maybe that's weird, but I have other friends with similar tattoos dedicated to being from here. One of our elders has a tattoo of a boat motor prop, Blackbeard's flag and a Doppler Radar image of a hurricane. We like being from here…a lot!

This seems to be a common mindset in small towns all over. Many people cannot wait to tell you how long they have lived in that particular town and it's easy to see that they get a sense of value from it.

How does that apply to ministry in small towns? Well, I benefit to an infinite degree from being from the small town where the church I lead is. However, there are plenty of difficulties as well. Practically everyone knows me and let's just say I didn't grow up imagining that I would someday lead a church here. If I had known that I would have done a lot of things differently.

However, being from here has helped me navigate the culture because I am truly part of it. I'm indigenous. There is even a book about our small town and my mom with my granddad is pictured on the front cover. I don't take it for granted that a lot of my ability to contextualize ministry comes directly from me being "from here."

Most of the staff and elders in our church, however, are not from here. There is an added challenge that comes from that. Each of them has had to earn credibility that was practically handed over to me. One of the interesting things I have witnessed as I have watched them work to build relationships and engage the culture is how intimidating it can be for them.

As much as local people like feeling like insiders, it clearly makes non-local people feel like outsiders. We have words for people who aren't from here. Words like, "ding-batter" and "dit-dot." You probably don't know what those words mean but you can probably guess they aren't good. This doesn't go far in trying to smooth the way for new relationships even though this is usually done in absolute fun.

It can be hard to be an outsider in a small town. But please hear me, if you are going to really do more than just attract the already churched crowd who just try anything new, you will have to commit yourself to learning the culture and earning the right to be heard. And you must be willing to not give up or quit because of difficulty or intimidation.

But how do you even begin to earn credibility with local people? You cannot change where you are from, and you shouldn't try to.

One of the easiest ways I can encourage someone

who finds themselves in a small town feeling like an outsider is to find a hobby that other local people share and do it with locals. Some of our elders have taken up fishing and hunting having no prior experience or desire to fish or hunt.

This is not as original as it may sound at first. Paul explained he would be willing to become like people to reach them:

> For though I am free from all, I have made myself
> a servant to all, that I might win more of them.
> To the Jews I became as a Jew, in order to win
> Jews. To those under the law I became as one
> under the law (though not being myself under the
> law) that I might win those under the law.
> -1 Corinthians 9:19-20

Paul said he was willing to be "as" someone who was much different than he was. What does that mean? It means he was willing to become like them, and it doesn't sound like that was always very easy for Paul.

He seems to indicate that sometimes it even felt like "serving" to do so. Paul came from a distinct culture that he loved and was proud of. It's costly to have to put that on the shelf and adapt to a new culture. But it was worth it if the gospel made its way into their hearts and lives through Paul spending time with them.

I haven't always lived in my hometown. There was about a decade where I lived far away from North Carolina's east coast. I lived for over four years in East Texas and though I tried to bring my salty culture with me, it didn't work and I had to adapt.

By the end of the four years, I was frequently wearing tight Wrangler cowboy-cut jeans, a cowboy hat and boots. I went two-stepping two nights a week at a local honky-tonk and went to rodeos whenever they came to town. I made a lot of friends with local people and was sad to move away at the end of my time there. The honky-tonk threw a going away party for me when I left.

After my time in East Texas, I lived for five years in Southern California. You couldn't get further from my rural upbringing than to put me in one of the largest cities in the world. I had to ditch the cowboy clothes eventually after failing to convince my California friends to take up two-stepping. But I was able to go back to surfing; something I had grown up loving. But surfing in Southern California is much different than in Eastern North Carolina. In North Carolina, we are highly relational and I found surfing in California oftentimes so competitive that it was hard to enjoy it. Eventually, I made friends in the water though, and again I was sad to leave when it came time to move back to my hometown and plant One Harbor. Hobbies can be an easy way to engage with people who you don't know or understand.

Another tip to earn credibility is to find out what drives local people nuts about outsiders and try not to do those things. Listen to people complain about tourists and outsiders and you can pick up on these cultural faux pas.

It can be as simple as always talking about how much better the food was in the big city or it can be more nuanced. Here, we hate when tourists litter on our beaches or in our water. We love the place we live in and don't like it being treated like a trash can. That may not be the case where you live, but there are things that drive locals crazy.

These things are offensive to local people. Acting in ways that they find offensive makes them struggle with liking or trusting you long before you have gotten to what you really actually came for; the gospel.

Simply, local people love where they live. You can win even the grouchiest of them over by loving it too. We will discuss this more in Chapter Seven.

Mindset #2: "Nothing Big Can Happen In A Small Town"

As much as small towns are loved by many of those who call them home and have so their entire lives, there is usually a "small town mentality" that produces a subconscious inferiority complex.

Small town residents can give in to feeling inferior to those in larger cities. They usually drive long distances to go to fancy restaurants, concerts, theme parks or museums.

Therefore, sometimes you find small town folks will have a mixed love-hate relationship with the cities that is very similar to how I think most city inhabitants view small towns, "they are a nice place to visit."

I cannot tell you how many times I've heard someone from our town remark of how much they like cities like Los Angeles, Raleigh, London, New York or other prominent large cities. But they always say, "I could never live there."

There is a love for the excitement and opportunity of

the big cities, but a fear or even disdain for the type of life that one would have if they lived there permanently.

Here's where this gets interesting. This mentality makes many people who live in small towns see their town's importance as meager in comparison to large cities. Because of this, many of the best entrepreneurs are tempted to leave small towns because there is a lack of drive to do new things where they live.

We have a town near us where we are planning to plant a site that's called Havelock. However, the locals often refer to it as "Have-not" because they feel it lacks any real appeal.

This is probably why some people stay in their small town forever because they like life the way it is. Others cannot wait to get out. I have found this to be both a massive challenge and opportunity in a small town.

Helping people dream big dreams for their small town is one of the largest challenges any church planter or pastor will face in a small town.

The challenge is getting them to see that God is big and whatever he does is big, even if where he does it is small. Know that you won't overcome this with one sermon. It will take a long time to change people's perception of what a big God can do in their small town. I have settled that I will have to keep saying this sort of thing over and over for decades.

The opportunity comes from how little people in a small town have seen real courageous entrepreneurship. People want to be part of something significant, even if they don't know they do. I have found a lot of fruit in calling people to lay down their petty dreams and run hard for Jesus. I have seen people step up to the plate when we have called them to leverage their lives for the sake of the gospel.

No one may have ever really done that in the town that you find yourself in. That is a massive opportunity! But understand that people will more than likely suffer from an inferiority complex that makes them risk averse. You will have to consistently fight that as you call them to dream as big as God does for your town. I'm often reminded of how God reveals himself to Jeremiah as able to do the impossible.

> Behold, I am the Lord, the God of all flesh.
> Is anything too hard for me?
> - Jeremiah 32:27

God is not just the God of the people who live in a larger context. He is the God of the people who live where you live. And nothing is too hard for him. Never let the size of the town be the determining factor for what God wants to do there.

Mindset #3: "New Is Bad; Old Is Good"

It's no secret that Christians in typical small towns view anything new as wrong and new church planters might be confronted with, "The last thing this town needs is another church."

I heard this before I moved back to start One Harbor. I was asked if I knew how many churches were already in this town. I did. But there were thousands of people in our tiny town, and tens of thousands in our county, who didn't go to church and those were the people I was coming for.

This mindset isn't limited to Christians and churches. Restaurants often are faced with this too. We've gone through multiple Thai restaurants in the last couple of years here because local people are risk averse to things not deep-fried. Pray for us!

Old is good and new is bad comes from many small town inhabitants loving their traditions too much. However, this cannot be overlooked and this mindset has huge ramifications on how we do ministry. Let me give you a few examples.

Multisite is something that's almost accepted worldwide. I've even seen it work in rural Africa and post-Christian England and yet I knew it was going to cause controversy when we started the first multisite campus here.

We did everything we could to try and avoid confusion, but it happened regardless. I even preached live for the first year at the new site each Sunday. Still, the rumors around town were that we had a church split and half the church had gone to Beaufort. That I was still preaching there weekly and that we were still partnering together in every way would have made this the most godly church split I've ever seen!

We are a couple of years past the first multisite campus and are now moving on to begin working towards our fourth location. In just the past couple of years, I have seen the confusion and hostility around multisite change drastically because we did it and pulled it off. Now, however, we want to leverage that and take it a step further.

I want to see if a video site would work here in a small town context. There's a lot of reasons for it, namely it will be a lot easier to multiply ourselves across our region to reach folks if we can pull video off here. However, I'm already cringing on the inside anticipating the rumors and misunderstandings that will potentially come out of us trying this. But it is still worth trying and if it works, then other churches in our area will be able to try it without nearly as much skepticism as we will get.

That's something that I think is valuable. We can afford to risk a little because our experiments benefit the next generation of church planters. Innovation must be something we consistently persist in if we are really on mission. However, change for the sake of change is dumb and dangerous. For a healthy understanding of how you can create a culture in your church where you can try new things without painting yourself in a corner, read Larry Osborne's "Sticky Leaders: The Secret To Lasting Change And Innovation."

What if video doesn't work? This is something I want to take a second to focus on. Not everything that works somewhere else will work where you are. That's ok. Some new things are worth trying and some are not. At the end of the day, if it's not resulting in more people meeting Jesus, ditch it and try something else.

We are so quick to spiritualize our models of church when it comes to mere techniques. This is silly. Just look back over our shoulders and see how many different ways have transpired before we arrived at what we have today. As quick as we should be to try something new, we should be equally as diligent at assessing to see whether or not the new initiative is sustainable.

Jesus used fishing as an analogy for reaching the lost. "Fishers of men" is what we are called to be. Fishermen use specific baits, luers, lines, depths, speeds, and so on to try and catch fish. If some bait that worked last time isn't working this time, a good fisherman tries something different. Be a good fisher of men. As someone once said, "try anything short of sin if it leads to people getting saved."

Finally, existing churches will probably offer a mixed response to your arrival. You can't blame them. They've seen this before...or so they think. I have hoped and prayed for amazing unity in our town amongst pastors and will continue to do so. Some of those relationships come easy and others do not. Let me give you some advice on how to at least create the opportunity for unity.

Don't ever talk bad about other churches. You will be tempted to, but don't give in. Don't seek out people who are at other churches who may be disgruntled and try to get them to join you. When, not if, people from other churches want to join you, ask them why and how they left their last church. I have had many conversations with people that led to a realization that they were leaving their previous church for poor reasons and needed to go back.

This won't guarantee that every other pastor will like you any more than it has for me, but it will pave the way for potential partnership in the future and you will be able to sleep at night, which is invaluable.

Not All Mindsets Are Worth Honoring

As much as there is to celebrate in small towns, there are some very unhelpful mindsets that still prevail. For instance, hatred towards people perceived to be different or wrong is not one of the things we should embrace or celebrate. Rather, attitudes like this must be challenged.

Racism, for example, is sadly something that still

prevails in many small towns. I know of towns near us where people of color are still afraid to go. That is not just a social problem, that's a gospel problem! That is the church's problem.

That in mind, we saw so many people coming to One Harbor from all walks of life...but they were basically all white. But our town is 77% white and 14% black. To be clear, I wasn't hoping for a completely 50/50 representation on Sundays because that's not what our town looks like. However, it was odd to me that we were seeing none of the 1,300 black people in our community join our church.

I believe it was connected to levels of conscious or subconscious racism. There were probably folks in our church who thought less of black people. They used racist jokes but wouldn't call themselves racists. There were also people who just liked the white church-black church norm that is seen in many small towns. I hate it.

I think some of that love for Sunday-segregation is even present in the black community in small towns. While I highly respect the complexity of our racial history, we cannot allow that to keep us from having the type of church that God wants to have on earth representing his Kingdom.

See, in eternity, we find out that all nationalities will be represented together before the throne of God worshipping the same Jesus. This is something we long for, but it also means something for us today.

Jesus told us that we should pray, "Your kingdom come, your will be done on earth as it is in heaven" (Matthew 6:10). Because in heaven we don't find racial divides, the church should fight to represent that on earth.

Convicted deeply by this, I was not content to have any level of racism present in our church, even though many perceived racism to be an unchangeable part of the culture. We set off to preach into this and I tried to work it in to almost every sermon for about a year and a half. People have begun to repent of racism and others are beginning to realize that a white church-black church culture shows those in our town who are not Christians that we really didn't want what God wants.

Recently, my oldest childhood friend, a black man, came to church for the first time. I was so excited. But as I met him in the lobby I could see him looking all over the room. I wondered what it was that was bothering him. He said, "You lead one of the biggest churches in this county Donnie, but where are all the black people?" We both laughed but I told him he was wrong. We don't have as many as we want to have, but we are a long way from where we were. I promptly introduced him to some of our dearest and best leaders, a black family who are helping us to not be an all white church. My friend has decided he wants to help us with that too.

This makes my heart melt. I hate racism because Jesus does. Our church has to push past this cultural problem that has become so normal...even on Sunday mornings.

I tell that story to help you see that you will need persistence and courage to tackle certain aspects of the culture you find yourself in, but it can be done.

Chapter Six Pop Quiz: How Well Do You Understand Your Town's Mindsets?

1. Good missionaries know which parts of the culture are redeemable and which ones must be rejected. A bad missionary worships everything the culture worships. Do you know the anti-gospel idols that your city worships? How are you challenging them with the gospel?

2. What mindsets mentioned in this chapter do you see in your small town?

3. What additional mindsets do you see represented in your small town?

4. A lazy missionary will gain all of his cultural assumptions by watching world news or hearing about what happens somewhere else. However, what people are feeling in your town may be much different. Do you think you are addressing relevant mindsets that need to be changed in your context or are you relying on a broad stroke approach that isn't derived from personally assessing people in your town?

5. Sometimes we perceive success as behavior change but we are wise to remember that many small towns have historically always been more predisposed to morality. But behavior change is not always because of heart change because morality is not the same as the gospel. Are action-producing mindsets something that has even entered your thought process as you seek to bring the gospel to your small town, or are you just focused on people changing their actions?

CHAPTER SEVEN

BEING A GOOD LOCAL

Talk to anyone who lives in a small town and they will tell you how they sometimes feel like they are living in a bubble. Everyone knows everything about you almost instantly. This can be very good or very bad. Your reputation really matters in a small town. It takes a lot of time to win a good reputation in a small town and only one bad decision to lose that reputation.

I've mentioned already how important it is to be considered a local resident in a small town and how those from the outside can work to be accepted by the locals. But just being a local isn't enough. A lot of your influence comes down to you being a good or bad local. Here are some ways I have learned to be a good local in my small town.

Learn To Enjoy Small Talk...Lots Of Small Talk

In a small town, usually people like to chitchat. Everywhere I went today, for instance, I saw numerous people who knew me and wanted to talk. That's everyday in a small town for me. The awkwardness comes from sometimes not knowing them and the fact that I seem to always have too much to do, but I politely chat because it is what you do in a small town. And these are people made in God's image and he loves them.

It seems like this is the same in small towns around the world. For instance, I have Zulu friends in South Africa who tell me that they are always late to meetings because they have to walk everywhere. I assumed that they were meaning it takes a long time to physically walk, but they clarified that it wasn't the walking that took so long. What caused their delay was the unwritten policy of having to have full conversations with everyone you meet along the way as you walk.

My small town upbringing caused me to instantly

identify deeply with my Zulu brothers and sisters. This is the normal day-to-day way of life in a small town but this can be a huge challenge if you come from a large city where there is no expectation to be personable to everyone you see.

My first experience in a big city was a trip to Boston. I remember being so offended that no one wanted to talk to me on the street. What I didn't know was that it wasn't as culturally appropriate to talk to random strangers everywhere like it is in the small town I come from. Looking back, I probably came across like an insane person walking around smiling and waving to people I had never seen before.

If making time for small talk is new to you, it will take some getting used to. Please take it from me that always acting like you have somewhere better to be will eventually lead you to unnecessarily offending residents in small towns. Just accept it as part of the culture and make the time to talk whenever you can, politely excusing yourself only when you really must.

Finally, you don't have to just put up with this aspect of small town life. You can use these conversations as opportunities to get to know people, find out what they care about, what they are afraid of, what they look forward to. This will only make you a better pastor and leader in a small town.

Shop Local As Much As Possible

One of my proudest moments as a church planter in this town might seem strange to you. It was when I received an honorary "staff" shirt from a local shop that has done a brilliant job of serving our city. The owners do not go to our church, but they are fantastic members of our community. I shop there as much as I can because of their quality and selection, but frankly there are other places I could go or I could just buy much of what they sell online. The real reason to support them is because they support our community. They love our town and I have come to love them.

In a small town, we work together to help each other out. It's true that in a small town, there may not be as many of the popular stores that you will find in large cities or even suburbs. This also means that you may not get the lowest price or even the widest selection when you try to shop local.

Your first instinct will be to schedule frequent drives to the big city to stock up on all your necessities and that's not a terrible thing. However, I would encourage you to see shopping local as an opportunity to become a good local. When small town locals see you shopping again and again at the same place they shop, they will begin to see you as part of the community.

Eat Local And Love Local Food

In our town, there are a variety of places to have breakfast. Coming back to my hometown from a large city, I found myself scheduling breakfasts with people at the newest chain restaurants in town. Those places are great and some of our best friends own fantastic franchise restaurants here. But what I noticed was that there were some people who didn't eat at those restaurants. They were the hard-core locals, who preferred to eat breakfast at one of the diners that has been a staple here since before I was born.

There's also a local drive-in in our town that hasn't changed a thing in 50 years, but everyday it's packed with locals and tourists waiting for the best shrimp burger you have ever had. Other burger joints come and go, but El's Drive-In is a staple that will hopefully be here until Jesus comes back.

What I am getting at is, no matter how great national

restaurant chains can be, small town people will always have a soft spot in their hearts for the food they grew up with. If you are going to really be seen as a local, you will have to occasionally frequent these restaurants too instead of only eating at the newest places in town. That said, here are a couple of additional things that you should consider when eating at a restaurant in a small town.

Firstly, be a great tipper. Sunday afternoons are dreaded shifts for wait staff because church-folk are notoriously bad tippers. Seriously. What is wrong with us? Please help reverse that. Be generous. Order one less appetizer so you can be a little extra generous if necessary. Write something kind on the receipt about how great the food or the service was. The next time you are in that restaurant ask for the same server. Build a relationship and treat them like a real person who has a life outside of bringing you more ice water. They have bigger problems in their life than the fact that your order came out wrong, and as a Christian, you should care about that.

Secondly, and this will take some restraint; never write a bad review about a restaurant in a small town. The apps on our phones make it easy to make a poor decision off the back of a bad experience at a restaurant. This is about as helpful as drunk-posting on Facebook at 2AM.

Good locals don't stoop to this level of low-grade-harassment. If you don't like the food, just don't come back. That's an adult way to handle it. You don't have to pretend to be a judge from some pretentious show on the Food Network. Plus, no matter how creative your screen name is, people in a small town will remember you and figure out who wrote the review. This is such an unnecessary reason to have local people hate you.

Eating local is far from just being about restaurants. What do you know about the indigenous food of your area? Where I'm from its seafood and pork. I recently spent time with a church planter who lives in a fishing community and made a confession; he's never had a soft shell crab. It took me a minute to find a bible verse to keep me from judging him. I eventually did. The thing is, it's not about eating a soft shell crab, but unless you're allergic to seafood, no one from here will understand why on earth you wouldn't eat a soft shell crab. We are obsessed with them.

Food means a lot to people. Native food has always been a means by which locals have celebrated life together and welcomed in outsiders.

When you are invited over for a "pig pickin" in my neck of the woods, you don't turn it down. If you are a vegan, God bless you, you will simply have a harder time engaging the culture here. When someone does invite you to come eat with them, give as many compliments as possible. Everyone likes to be told their food tastes great. Turning your nose up and asking if they know how many calories are in the home-made pie are not going to lead to a second invite or to people opening up their hearts to you.

Don't Be A Jerk

I'm not saying that everyone who lives in a big city is a jerk. But I lived in Los Angeles and Orange County for five years and I did notice a propensity to act like the people you inter-act with in restaurants and stores are not people you will ever see again. What this leads to is a couple of unhelpful patterns for ministry that cause problems in a small town.

Firstly, when you don't think you will ever see wait staff or store staff again, you don't naturally make any effort to get to know them. This means you don't really take any time to engage them. However, this is much different than in a small town where you will find yourself constantly bumping into these people again and again. So, in a small town, you should take every opportunity to be kind and courteous.

The second propensity is way worse. Because you don't think you are ever going to see them again it's easier to be demanding and to get ugly with people when they don't do what you want. If they get your food order wrong or you don't get the level of customer service you want, many people in a large city feel the freedom to be a jerk about it. This may be common in a large city, although I wouldn't recommend it since those people need kindness too.

However, in a small town, this will bite you really quick. If I was to scream at a waitress for messing up my order where I live, my whole town would probably hear about it before the night was over. Not only would everyone find out, but people would be disappointed in me because that's just not how you treat people. No doubt about it, I would have people leave our church or never even come because of how I treated this waitress.

Here's a story to illustrate this. My wife and I wanted to buy a boat for a long time so we could enjoy the uninhabited islands all around us any time we wanted. We searched and searched for a good deal. Finally we found one that we liked in a tiny rural community nearby. We pulled up to look at the boat finding the seller in his yard very upset.

He was a shrimper and truck driver who lived in a glorified trailer in the woods and his walker coonhounds were yelping so loud you could hardly think. I couldn't help but ask why he was so upset.

A man, he explained, from a large city a few hours from us, had just driven down to look at his boat. The man spent the entire time talking about how nice his home is in the big city and how every night he drinks red wine while staring at his new Mercedes. About the time this man made it to the part of the story where he bragged about all the boats he already owned, the shrimper had had enough. The boat seller told me he had thrown him off his property because he didn't want to sell his boat to a…well, you can fill in the blanks.

The point of this story is that we ended up with a great deal on an awesome boat and the other guy didn't. We took time to get to know the man who was selling the boat and talked about his life. We cared about him more than getting his boat. I even brought him some fish I had spear-fished after I bought the boat. We wanted a good deal, but we weren't willing to be jerks to get it. He could tell the difference. Most people can.

Don't Be An Outlaw

My childhood friends reading this will have a good laugh at my expense because I had been pulled over by the police 24 times before I graduated high school. No, I didn't drive a sports car. I drove a three-cylinder Daihatsu hatchback. It had the horsepower of a lawn mower but that didn't stop me from driving it like a Porsche. I even remember being pulled over three times in a nine-mile stretch on the same night.

Why the trip down memory lane? Well, when I came back home to plant a church it hit me one day that police officers might one day attend the church I was leading; which they now do. How awkward would it be if I was the resident speed-demon and yet apparently a pastor?

Additionally, what message would I send by speeding and breaking the law? I would be communicating that I don't really care about our city as much as I said I did because I was willing to endanger others just because I was in a hurry. This has been enough for me to keep a reign on my aggressive driving and to date I have not received a ticket since I have been back.

The point is that how you act is as important as what you say especially when you live in the fishbowl that small towns often feel like. Don't make the mistake of ruining your reputation over something trivial before you ever get a chance to tell someone about Jesus.

Be A Blessing

Recently, the police called one of the pastors at our church and said there was a woman who has small children and is trying to escape an abusive relationship. The fact that the police called us to help with that is something I love about our church.

This is not the first time something like that has happened. We frequently have the privilege to serve hurting and marginalized people in our town because the word is out that we really care.

When a tornado came through the middle of our

town, we cancelled our Sunday services and were some of the first climbing on roofs with chainsaws and clearing debris. Every time a hurricane hits us, we shut down for days to serve our community. Recently, after a bad storm, I came across a highway patrol officer who was trapped in his car surrounded by water on a flooded street. I nearly broke my back pushing him out until a few other guys came to help.

This is not meant in the slightest to be a pat on our own backs and this is not Special Forces Christianity. This is what the church was meant to do. We are here to be a blessing. That goes beyond just preaching good messages and having a good kids ministries. The entire community should flourish because we are there living for Jesus. This goes back to God's charge to Abraham in Genesis 12:1-3:

> Now the Lord said to Abram, "Go from your country and your kindred and your father's house to the land that I will show you. And I will make of you a great nation, and I will bless you and make your name great, so that you will be a blessing. I will bless those who bless you, and him who dishonors you I will curse, and in you all the

families of the earth shall be blessed.

God has sent us to the towns we live in to be a blessing. This is why we should seek to be the best locals we can be. We should want to be the pastor that everyone jokes should be mayor. Not because we dress up really nice all the time, but because it is perceived that we love our town and we want it to thrive.

I was recently named one of our county's eight most influential leaders. The article made me weep because it was all about how our church has loved this city and it showed that people wanted us to stay.

When considering how you can engage the culture of your small town with the gospel, please don't just settle for contextualized church programs and church facilities. Love where you live and serve where you live. Let everyone know that you really care about them, whether they come to your church or not. Let integrity, generosity and compassion be something the whole town cannot escape when they are around you or the folks in your church.

Chapter Seven Pop Quiz: Are You A Good Or Bad Local?

1. Do you frequently shop where local people do and eat where they eat? If not, what message do you think that is sending to the people in your small town?

2. Do you think that the way you act when you don't receive good customer service is helping or hurting your ability to be a good local?

3. Do people think that you wish you lived somewhere else, maybe where you used to live before? What evidence have you given to show that you are content where God has placed you? Have you joined any clubs or sporting teams? Have you bought a home? I mention that last one because renting can often be seen as hedging your bets or keeping one foot in and one foot ready to leave when this gets too difficult. I don't mean that if it's financially unwise you should still buy a home. I just want you to consider how you can communicate a long-term commitment to the place you are ministering in.

4. Do people love that you are in their town? Do they see the value you bring? Or do you come across as someone who is only there to take from them? Have you had any interactions with city officials where they have reached out to you for help? What about when you have contacted the city, is it only to get something like a favor or a permit or have you approached them to see how your church can serve and be a blessing If you haven't already, how can you love and serve your city with no strings attached?

CHAPTER EIGHT

HOW BIG CITY CHURCHES CAN HELP SMALL TOWNS

The reality is that not everyone who reads this will be called to lead a church in a small town. Thankfully, God will call many of us to go to the big cities and labor there. But how can we do better than we have done thus far? How can we put an end to the separation and comparisons of which places are more important than others? Why would big city churches want to partner with small town churches?

I think it would be helpful for us to consider how the bible shows God working in his mission. What we see from the beginning of creation is that God loves collaboration that leads to mission.

God said, "Let us make…" and then he made his creation in such a way that each organism depends on and serves other organisms. Later we learn that God's church is a house made of living stones. We learn that we are each uniquely made but are knit together as part of one body. God couldn't be clearer that he wants us to collaborate together.

What do we do instead? We live in silos, clustered up in our cliques with those just like us. We pretend that someone in a context different to us is not as important or necessary. That's clearly not what collaboration and partnership looks like. Well then, what does it look like?

Practically, it looks like humbly acknowledging we need each other. Remember, like the wall that Nehemiah built, whether it is the valley gate or dung gate, both were equally needed. And what we are building, if it is indeed the Kingdom of God, will outlast all of us. But how do we build such meaningful partnerships?

First, we need to be realistic. You can't partner with everyone. But you can and should partner with someone. And you can probably do a lot more partnering with others than you think you can. My friend PJ Smyth loves to quote the African proverb, "If you want to go fast, go alone. If you want to go far, go together." This is exactly what I'm getting at.

There are people who you can connect with on every necessary level and those people form primary partnerships. But there are other people who you differ with on lesser issues that you can still learn a lot from, love and serve. Most of us only engage with the former. We are not interested in learning from anyone outside of our "tribe."

Real collaboration, however, starts where every godly initiative does; in the heart. We need our hearts to be convinced that we don't have everything we need. We need to learn from other workers in this "field" who can help us do our job better.

Many city churches simply need to see the larger mission in their state. No state is comprised solely of large cities. Think of the state you live in right now. Countless small towns and rural areas are actually everywhere once you look for them.

Like I said earlier, a win in the city and a loss in the small towns isn't a win from a Kingdom standpoint. The opposite is true as well. We need to be advancing the gospel well in every corner of the world because it is the field to which we were sent by Jesus.

But practically, how can we really partner together? I think it looks something like guys with an apostolic gifting (small "a") in large cities to get a heart to serve and work with guys with an apostolic (small "a") gifting in small towns and vice versa. When the heart is there, you have a real recipe for collaboration. When we realize we actually need each other, we will figure out how to serve each other.

Collaboration Killers

What are the fastest ways to kill any kind of godly collaboration? Here are the things that come to mind as I consider what I've seen and experienced.

Imperialism

It's sad to say, but if a pastor of a large church from a big city near me with a ton of momentum engaged me out of nowhere, I'd assume that he was wanting to make our church one of his sites. That's because this happens…a lot. And it's not ok.

What it does is reinforce the negative stereotype that big city people have no real value for small towns if it doesn't directly benefit them. This is what people fear the most about large cities. "If they are here, they are here to take over."

So, if you lead a church in a large city and God leads you to begin looking to serve churches in small towns around you, run to this tension and over-communicate that you are not interested in taking over, just serving. That may lead, in some cases, to mergers, but that shouldn't be the first thing in our minds.

I've so benefited from our relationship with Vintage Church in Raleigh. They have only sought to be a blessing to us. We are growing more and more in our love and mutual respect for each other and are seeing increasing ways that we can serve each other.

I have experienced this at an overwhelming level with my friends at other large city churches like Frontline Church in Oklahoma City. I'm telling you, it's a beautiful thing. It is something of what God is communicating when he says that he blesses brothers dwelling together in unity (Psalm 133). I am praying for a lot more of that for us and for those reading this book.

Context Pride

A guy on our team here at One Harbor is always reminding me that when we go into impoverished neighborhoods, we aren't just there to serve, we are there to learn from them too. There is something beautiful happening in every context if we will look for it.

This is a huge lesson for us in large cities or small towns who are looking to collaborate. We are naturally bent towards thinking that our context is better or right. We must both watch out for this. We should see that there is a ton we can learn from each other and always be quick to point that out. That's called humility and it is godly.

Unrealistic Expectations

On the back of reading this you may be tempted to rush out and promise every church planter in a small town near you that you will do anything you can to help them. I would caution you against that. Just start somewhere. Word will spread that you care, are humble and helpful.

This was already mentioned earlier but let's get a little more practical. When, not if, pastors call you for help, they will probably ask you this, "How do you guys do your _____ ministry?" You should do your best to refuse to answer that question. Here's why. When it comes to answering their question, you do _____ as a result of a good process of reading your context and the climate of your church, that will be different for them. You are also a different leader and have a different team.

The differences between you and them are endless; therefore it is highly likely that the outcomes should be different. Also, you are not helping them by giving them this answer, you are making them dependent on you. This kind of co-dependent relationship will make collaboration unsustainable.

So, rather say, "I'll tell you what, ask me 'Why we did what we do?' not how." Force them to go through the same process which will help them become a better leader and will also help them avoid the consequences of pasting something into their context that will end poorly.

As a pastor of a church in a large city, you will not be able to help everyone ministering in small towns around you, but with intentionality and a heart to serve, you will be able to invest into some. My guess is that, in doing so, you will learn from them as well.

CONCLUSION

SMALL TOWNS ARE MORE STRATEGIC THAN WE THINK

Important people are often born in unimportant places. Jesus, to the surprise of many in his day, was born in a town that was tiny and insignificant. Billy Graham was born in a small town outside of Charlotte, NC. Brad Pitt, Britney Spears and many other influential celebrities were born in small towns.

Additionally, US Presidents Harry Truman, Dwight Eisenhower, Lyndon Johnson, Richard Nixon, Jimmy Carter, Ronald Reagan, George Bush Sr, George W. Bush and Bill Clinton were all born in small towns. That's every President except John F. Kennedy, Gerald Ford and Barack Obama in the last 70 years.

Consider the following important questions as we look at a world that is drastically changing and will require extreme courage to lead in the future: What if we had great churches in all of these towns? How much different could the lives of these leaders have been? And, for us, if we take small town ministry seriously now, can we help shape the future?

Please hear this, you and I will never know where the future leaders will be born. Strategic people are not just born in large cities. When we consider the future implications, we realize small town ministry must be taken as seriously as ministry anywhere else.

I am trusting God for an army of churches to be planted in small towns and for countless others to hear a call to revitalization. Additionally, I'm praying for pastors in large cities to look for ways to encourage and equip church planters and existing pastors in small towns.

If you, after reading this book, want to know more or would like to join us in this endeavor, please visit us at www.smalltownjesus.com.